FIRST N
FAITH
AND
ECOLOGY

Freda Rajotte

Anglican Book Centre
Toronto, Ontario

United Church Publishing House
Etobicoke, Ontario

CASSELL

Cassell
Wellington House, 125 Strand, London WC2R 0BB, UK

Anglican Book Centre   United Church Publishing House
600 Jarvis Street   3250 Bloor Street West, Fourth Floor
Toronto, Ontario   Etobicoke, Ontario
M4Y 2J6 Canada   M8X 2Y4 Canada

© Freda Rajotte 1998

All rights reserved. No part of this publication may be reproduced or transmitted in any form or by any means, electronic or mechanical including photocopying, recording or any information storage or retrieval system, without prior permission in writing from the publishers.

First published 1998

British Library Cataloguing-in-Publication Data
A catalogue record for this book is available from the British Library.

ISBN 0-304-70312-5

Extracts from *Black Elk Speaks* are used by permission of the University of Nebraska Press.
Navajo Night Chant on pages 83–4, from *Native American Traditions*, edited by Sam D. Gill, is used by permission of Wadsworth Publishing Co.

Cover illustration: *The Dreaming*, painting by Freda Rajotte.
Typeset by Kenneth Burnley at Irby, Wirral, Cheshire.
Printed and bound in Great Britain by Biddles Ltd, Guildford and King's Lynn.

FIRST NATIONS FAITH AND ECOLOGY

Also available:

WORLD RELIGIONS AND ECOLOGY

This series looks at how each of several world religions has treated ecology in the past, what the teaching of each has to say on the subject, and how that is applied today. Contributors from a variety of backgrounds in each religion put forward material for thought and discussion through poetry, stories and pictures as well as ideas and theories.

The series is sponsored by the World Wide Fund for Nature, who believe that a true understanding of our relation to the natural world is the best step towards saving our planet.

Titles in the series are:

BUDDHISM AND ECOLOGY
*Martine Batchelor
and Kerry Brown*

CHRISTIANITY AND ECOLOGY
*Elizabeth Breuilly
and Martin Palmer*

HINDUISM AND ECOLOGY: Seeds of Truth
Ranchor Prime

ISLAM AND ECOLOGY
*Fazlun M. Khalid
with Joanne O'Brien*

CONTENTS

	Preface	vii
1	LIVING THE SACRED STORY	1
2	CREATION	7
3	THE SACRED CIRCLE OF LIFE	21
4	ANIMALS ARE SACRED	35
5	THE BROKEN HOOP	45
6	MENDING THE HOOP	55
7	HEALING THE SPIRIT	67
8	THE LAND: RAVAGE, REPATRIATION AND RESURRECTION	87
9	FAITH AND VISION	99
10	CHIEF SEATTLE'S SPEECH	107
	Notes	112
	References	113
	Bannock: A Traditional First Nations Food	117

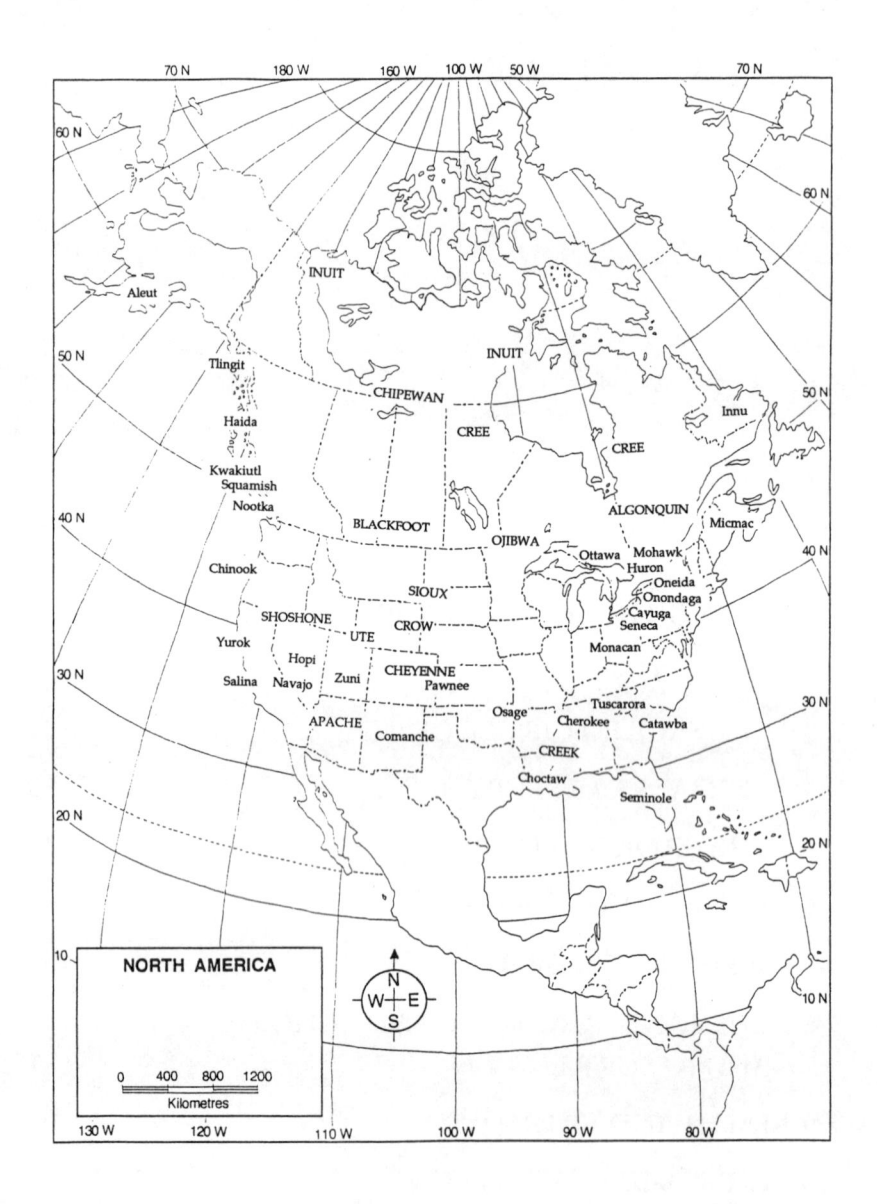

Map showing the location of major tribal groups or nations mentioned in the text

PREFACE

This book began several years ago during discussions in a publishing house in London, England. A series of books had been produced on major world faiths and ecology. We in CCEER (Canadian Coalition for Ecology, Ethics and Religion) felt very strongly that any such series would only be appropriate in North America if it began with a volume on First Nations Faith and Ecology. Thus the work on this book began.

CCEER works on the principle that each faith should speak for itself, but in a way that makes their teaching accessible to people of other faiths and to those of a secular world.

The cultures, languages, lifestyles and religious beliefs and practices of the First Nations peoples of North America are so diverse that this appeared to be a daunting task. Each group requires individual study because each is a separate people with their own language, mythology and traditions. Almost all have been the subject of numerous studies and publications dealing with every aspect of their culture. This book makes no pretensions at trying to be comprehensive, but only to be representative of that diversity. In the course of several years during which this material was selected and compiled we contacted many Native Elders, and university departments of Native Studies. We listened to teachings and stories around many campfires and kitchen tables, attended sweat lodges, and Sun Dances and other ceremonies. Everywhere we found people willing to share with us their stories and information and answer our questions.

The material that follows is an attempt to compile some of this information, to simplify and draw some generalizations from an overwhelming complexity, while respecting the integrity and distinctiveness of each and every culture.

ACKNOWLEDGEMENTS

We are extremely grateful to: Teresa Altiman, who consented to provide the wonderful illustrations for this book; David Bosnich, graduate research student at the Natural Resources Institute, University of Manitoba, for his assistance in research and correspondence; Laverne V. Jacobs, Co-ordinator Native Ministries, Anglican Church of Canada.

We acknowledge the invaluable help and suggestions and resource material from three readers: The Very Revd Dr Stan McKay Sr, respected Elder, and former Moderator of the United Church of Canada; Ms Lisa Hill, Assembly of Manitoba Chiefs; Dr Jennifer Brown, lecturer in Native History, University of Winnipeg.

Grateful acknowledgement is made both to the Alliance of Religions and Conservation (ARC) of the UK and to the United Church of Canada for their support and also for their continued encouragement throughout this project.

Among the many who willingly shared information and helped with this project we would like to thank in particular: Dr Shirley Williams, Department of Native Studies, Trent University; Clayton Sandy, Winnipeg; Suzie Berneshawi, Halifax; Donna Billy, Squamish; Chief Jerry Fontaine, Manitoba; Alvin Manitopes, Edmonton, Alberta; Dave Courchene, Seven Sisters, Manitoba; Art and Ngomis Solomon, Ontario; Martha Johnson, Yellowknife; Irene Sullivan, Golden, Colorado; Wayne A. Holst, Arctic Institute, University of Calgary; George Tinker, Iliff School of Theology; Carl Bird, Peguis, Manitoba; Sylvia and Eugene Denny, Cape Breton; Dan Thomas, Department of Native Education, Winnipeg; Pete Enrick, Ranklin Inlet, NWT; Phillip J. McKay, Gwai Band, Northern BC; Revd Laverne Jacobs, Toronto; Professor Fikret Berkes, University of Manitoba.

While every care has been taken in compiling the following material, all opinions expressed in this book remain the sole responsibility of the author.

*Sacred eagle feather,
tobacco in a piece of cloth and sweetgrass braided into a hoop*

O Great Spirit,
Whose voice we hear in the winds,
and whose breath gives life to the world,
hear us! We are small and weak,
we need your strength and wisdom.

May we walk in beauty.
May our eyes
    ever behold the red and purple sunset.

May our hands respect the things you have made
    and our ears be sharp to hear your voice.

Make us wise so that we may understand the things
    you have taught our people.

Help us learn the lessons you have hidden
    in every leaf and rock.

Make us always ready to come to you
    with clean hands and straight eyes.

So when life fades, as the fading sunset,
    our spirits may come to you without shame.

Traditional Native American prayer

1 | LIVING THE SACRED STORY

Somewhere between 40,000 and 30,000 years ago the first humans arrived in the Americas. Though the exact date is still disputed by scholars, it is known that numerous migrations continued to come from northern China across the Bering Strait land bridge between 30,000 BP (before the present) and 14,000 BP, when melting glaciers raised the sea level several hundred feet, and the Bering land bridge was submerged.

During this long period of time every part of the Americas was settled. This settlement certainly had an impact on the surrounding environment, for example the area of open prairie grassland was increased by the regular use of fire. There is also evidence of pueblo settlements in the dry southwest of the United States having been abandoned long before European arrival, apparently owing to environmental deterioration when the trees had been removed from the surrounding hills for use. Yet the impact of human settlement over these many thousands of years was very small compared to the rapid damage that we are causing at the present time.

> Indigenous people occupied the land for thousands of years before contact with Europeans. During this period of pre-contact, our ancestors developed ways and means of relating to each other and to the land, based upon a very

simple and pragmatic understanding of their presence on this earth. If they failed to consider what the environment had to offer, how much it could give, and at what times it was prepared to do this – they would simply die. This basic law held for every living thing on earth. All living creatures had to be cognizant of the structure of the day, the cycles of the seasons and their effects on all other living matter. If the plant world tried to grow in the winter, it would die, the earth was not prepared to give life at this time. If the animal world did not heed the changing of the seasons and prepare themselves, by leaving the immediate environment for a more hospitable one or by storing fat for the winter, they would die. If the people were to deplete the animal or plant resources of their immediate environment, pain and suffering could be expected. This understanding gave rise to a relationship that is intimately connected to the sustainability of the earth and its resources.

(Clarkson, Morrissette and Regallet, p. 4)

Thus over many thousands of years the First Nations Peoples developed ways of living in harmony with the natural world and with their neighbours. Concern for the well-being of the community as a whole and compliance with natural law were not a matter of achieving some ideal but, rather, were necessities that constituted the very basis for human survival.

As many as 300 different First Nations languages were spoken at the time of the first European contact. In this book we will try to honour the richness and diversity of teachings, practices, ways of life, mythologies and rituals of some of the hundreds of cultures in Native North America – the region from Northern Mexico to the Arctic Circle. As today's dominant perspective draws its roots from thousands of years of cultural diversity, migration and evolution, so also does Indigenous history. However, it is possible to make some generalizations.

The roots of First Nations culture go back for thousands of years to the time of the very first migrations of small bands of people into North America. Values and beliefs were handed on from one generation to the next, together with the skills needed for hunting and farming, fishing and food storage, building and carving, sewing and child care. Legends and stories, myths of origins were generally told around the fires, and were kept for winter seasons of the year. 'The tradition of these cultures – the forms and substances that give each culture its identity and vitality – are transmitted through stories and rites; indeed mythology and ritual constitute the traditions of a culture' (Gill and Sullivan, p. xi).

Unfortunately during much of the last 500 years, the First Nations

Peoples have had to contend with the arrival of increasing numbers of settlers. Initially their numbers suffered a drastic decrease due to the fatal impact of the newly arrived European diseases such as influenza and smallpox. Later many communities were removed from their lands by the superior military numbers and weapons of the settlers. Some groups, such as the Beothuk of Newfoundland, were totally eliminated by genocide, and have disappeared for ever, together with their languages, wealth of experience, culture, beliefs and heritage.

For many others their first contact with people of European ancestry was with Christian missionaries. Thus today a great many First Nations Peoples are Christians, and a few belong to other world faiths such as Islam and Baha'i. Throughout North America, Christian religion and the lifestyle and values of immigrant North Americans, such as materialism, consumerism and individualism, have had a significant impact upon the present Native American way of life. Much of this influence has led to a change in world view, and many sources of stories, mythology and rituals bear the imprint of non-Native Americans.

Over the past several generations, pressure from missionaries and governments led to most Native rituals and ceremonies – such as the West Coast potlatch, the healing circle, sweat lodge, the use of sacramental peyote and even 'smudging' or the burning of sweetgrass – being banned and made illegal. Some ceremonies, rituals and stories have disappeared for ever. Only in the last few decades of the twentieth century has mainstream scholarship had a more open and accepting view of traditional cultures.

Despite half a millennium of suppression, and attempts at elimination, genocide and mass removal, now, at the end of the twentieth century, First Nations populations are increasing rapidly. Despite all attempts at assimilation, there has been an amazing renaissance in culture; and following decades of suppression, an incredible renewal and resurgence in spiritual teachings, practices and rituals. The last three decades of the twentieth century have been a time of awakening, reclaiming what was lost, and demanding justice. Impoverished tribes looked to the law courts to uphold ancient treaties that guaranteed vast lands would be reserved for ever for their exclusive use. Over 300 groups in the USA have achieved recognized tribal status, which makes them 'sovereign political bodies', with jurisdiction over their own reserve lands and all who live on them.

Not only is there a renewed interest in restoring the old ways and retrieving the lost ceremonies and mythologies that give meaning to life and that restore cultural and personal pride; there is also a generosity that wishes to share this wisdom and teaching that has been developed, collected, preserved and passed on from the ancestors since ancient time. The desire to share this wisdom and respect for the Earth is seen as being very urgent because of the rate at which the environment is being polluted and destroyed.

There is a growing awareness that we, in North America, are no longer living in a state of balance with nature, but are destroying the Earth's resources upon which we all depend for survival. When we look across the North American prairies today, and remember the vast herds of buffalo that once thundered over the plains, or gaze up into the empty skies that were once darkened with passenger pigeons, we may well ask how our society could have thoughtlessly destroyed so much so quickly. Our present, consumerist way of life cannot continue for ever, for it is consuming and destroying the ecologic base upon which our survival depends. This destruction is easy to ignore, because it is occurring on such a vast scale that it appears to be approaching very slowly, and is reported in a series of unrelated environmental disasters in the press and on the television. Here a forest is cut, somewhere else a lake is polluted with acid rain or mercury, rivers are dammed, oil spills spread across beaches and kill wildlife, deserts advance, crops fail, people starve.

As this destructiveness becomes increasingly apparent, more people are turning to the traditional teachings and wisdom of the First Nations, hoping to learn how to live in closer harmony with nature and with the spiritual realms. So let us listen respectfully to the teachings of the First Nations Peoples, who lived in North America for many thousands of years before the arrival of the first European settlers began.

As Buffy Sainte-Marie, a Plains Cree, states:

> We, the Indigenous people of the western hemisphere, who live on reservation communities, we see the destruction first because most of us live on the nuclear front-line; but you will see it soon. We are already decimated because of destructive environmental loopholes, whereby the political friends of the big energy companies allow the money junkies of the world to bulldoze and divert, strip mine and pollute, and dump toxic waste into the rivers in our communities . . . because they can get away with it . . . WAKE UP WORLD:

> ... this is not some tug-of-war over a real estate deal; this is a matter of life and death, for we are part of the environment.
>
> (Preface to Manitopes et al., *Voice of the Eagle*)

Ceremonies are performed for a specific purpose – to cure, to prepare for hunting, to assure agricultural fertility, to bring in another season or New Year, or to help individuals move along to another stage in the cycle of life. When such ceremonies are recorded in written form and out of context, the power inherent in them is almost always lost or obscured, so that they may appear as mere folk traditions or even as superstition.

> In fact rituals are the form, the crystallization, of the mythological and religious cycles that not only make sense of the cosmos, but in fact reveal, augment, and even bring about human beings' harmony with it. Without ritual, the tribal tradition has no formal expression, and ceases to exist except as a matter of bloodlines and transmitted stories.
>
> (Versluis, p. 48)

Certainly the stories and teachings given by the elders today are different from the stories and teachings of 500 years ago, for no part of any culture is without change. Traditionally they were passed down verbally from storyteller to storyteller, from elder to elder, and experienced some degree of change from one generation to the next. Indeed many myths and rituals are still powerful today precisely because they can be adapted and applied to changing situations. While this present book draws upon the ancient wisdom of the First Nations, it is not so much concerned with historic authenticity as with modern relevance. It focuses upon today's living First Nations faiths and what they have to teach people.

Thomas Yellowtail, Sun Dance chief of the Crow tribe, claims there is little use in mourning rituals now lost, and says:

> Modern Indians care little for spiritual things and traditional ways, so there are very few traditional people remaining with real medicine or understanding. Modern civilization has no understanding of sacred matters. Everything is backwards. This makes it even more important that young people follow what is left today. Even though many of the sacred ways are no longer with us, what we have left is enough for anyone, and if it is followed, it will lead as far as the person can go.
>
> (Yellowtail, p. 188)

2 | CREATION

People have a natural curiosity, and some of the most basic questions that they ask are about how the world began, what is the purpose of existence, and how we came to be here. Through the centuries people of every culture have been puzzled by these questions, and have attempted to answer them. Our answers will say a lot about how we perceive the world, society and ourselves, what we believe our relationship should be with other people and with the world around us. That is to say, our perception of the world and of our place in it is basic to our value system.

Every society has its stories and mythologies to answer these questions, and our own society is no exception. Sometimes we may find that the dominant, scientific world-view is in conflict with the creation stories of different religions. However, each fulfils a slightly different purpose. Science is generally concerned with attempting to answer the questions 'How' and 'When' the world came into being. As science has developed ever more powerful tools, and acquired increasing information from physics, optics and mathematics, it is able to date the origins of the solar system and of our planet with increasing accuracy. It can also tell us in more detail exactly how each stage of the evolution of our planetary system took place.

Religion, on the other hand, uses mythology and storytelling to deal with questions of meaning and purpose. It attempts to answer the questions of 'Why' we are here and what our relationship should be to the world and the people around us. From all over the world creation stories tell us that to be human is to be a creature of the Earth. In Genesis, for example, humans are formed 'from the dust of the ground'.

> Myths and rituals may be thought of as tools used by human beings to create and maintain community, health, identity, family and self. . . . Almost no recorders have appreciated the fact that a story or a ritual only really exists in its application. . . . (Unfortunately) most of the published records of myth and ritual present the stories and rituals without their histories and without their applications.
>
> (Gill and Sullivan, pp. xii, xiii)

Most First Nations cultures recount stories about the beginning of the world and how it gained its present shape and character. Often these stories go on to account for the creation of people, plants and animals. Frequently they account for and support the social, tribal and clan structure, outlining people's responsibility to the community as a whole and to the animals, plants and land. Some even tell of the origins of such attributes as hunger, sleep, disease and evil.

Although different creation stories exist with each tribe and cultural group, they tend to fall into several general types:

1. The Earth Diver

In these stories various animals or people attempt to dive to the bottom of the primordial waters and bring back a piece of mud from the bottom. Usually many animals fail before one finally succeeds. The mud that they bring back is used to create the Earth.

2. The World Parent

The simple example of Mother Earth and Father Sky rarely occurs in tribal cultures, but is more frequently referred to in contemporary Native American spirituality, and is probably a recent development that has arisen from cross-cultural influence. However, many creation stories, especially from the southwestern USA, feature a powerful sky god or celestial creator such as the Zuni Sun Father (Yatokka taccu) and the Moonlight Giving Mother.

3. The Emergence

Numerous creation myths weave stories around the theme of a journey through the underworlds. Eventually people, animals and plants emerge onto the present Earth. These stories are common in the south-western USA, but are also found in the southeast and among the Plains tribes.

4. Two Creators

In numerous other stories two legendary figures occupy the central creation role. Often they are warrior twins, but in other legends are sisters, or father and son, even nephew and uncle. Co-operation and also disagreements between the two result in the eventual shape of the world we see today, together with its good and evil characteristics.

5. Sacred Animals Create People

Many people, all shamans (or healers), and in some cases entire tribes or communities enjoy a very close and reciprocal relationship with a particular animal or other creature. It will be regarded with respect, and will become the central mythological figure in stories of origin. For example, among the north-west coastal people Raven is responsible for the arrival of humans. A story common in the south of California tells how it is Spider that spins and weaves the foundations of the Earth with its web of life, and serves as the first being.

Following are examples of some of the best-known and loved creation stories that illustrate each of these five major types. Although these five and many other creation stories differ, one tenet almost universally accepted was that all living things – plants as well as animals – shared the same origins as people. All were animated by the same spiritual life force and were to be treated with proper respect and consideration.

1. TURTLE ISLAND AND SKY WOMAN[1]
A Cree creation story

Muskrat dived down

North America is called Turtle Island in the teaching of many Native nations across the continent.

After the Creator had made the world with all the animals and with the first people, he told Wisakedjak, the Trickster, to take good care of the people, show them how to live and stop them from quarrelling with each other. However,

Wisakedjak delighted in playing tricks upon the animals and the people so that they became angry with each other, quarrelled and fought until the land was red with blood.

The Creator became so angry that he sent a flood to wash the Earth clean again. For many days the water rose until there was no land to be seen at all. Then Sky Woman fell down from the sky world, holding seeds from the Tree of Light. There was nowhere for her to land as the Earth was covered in water. As she fell, Ducks caught her on their wings, and landed Sky Woman gently in the world of water. When Turtle saw what had happened, she offered her body for Sky Woman's resting place.

Wisakedjak tried in vain to find a small piece of Earth for he did not have the power to create anything, but could expand what already existed. So he sent down one animal after another to try to reach the Earth beneath the flood waters. Otter tried several times but could not reach the bottom. Then Beaver tried, but he too was unable to dive deep enough to reach the land. Finally little Muskrat dived, down and down into the water, deeper and deeper. When he floated back to the surface he was dead, but clutched tightly between his paws were bits of earth. This earth was spread out over Turtle's back, and became a home for the first mother. There she planted the seeds from the Sky World.

The Turtle also has special knowledge and power because it can live both in water and on land. In this Cree creation story, Sky Woman is attributed with the power of re-creation. She breathes new life into the handful of earth Muskrat and the other animals died for, and restores all the plants and animals that drowned in the great flood.

This story is used to teach the value of co-operation and sacrifice for the good of the community, our dependence upon the other beings in the Creation, and the special re-creating powers of women.

First Nations Faith and Ecology

2. THE CREATION OF THE WORLD[2]
A Dakota-Sioux creation story

Sacred Navajo figures depicted in 50-year-old tapestry. Mother Earth, source of plants and life, and Father Sky, with the Milky Way shown in a chain of xxs and constellations, are identical in shape and size, since they are the two halves of the whole creation.

Wakan Tanka (the Creator), the Great Mystery who is timeless, envisioned the universe into existence, although it took eons of time for the Earth and people to evolve and assume their present shape. At first everything was drifting in the mists of space. Then Wakan Tanka created the first superiors.

So, in the beginning, Inyan (the stone god) found himself all alone in Chaos, a primeval darkness without substance or form. As Inyan grew lonely, he caused his powers to flow outward, forming Maka (the Earth), a goddess. Inyan's blood flowed upon the Earth, dried up and became hard rock. Shkan (sky) was then formed by more of Inyan's flowing blood.

Because Maka was naked and cold, still surrounded by darkness, Inyan released Anpao (dawn), a red light that cast no heat or shadow. Shkan then joined his power to Maka's to create a large shining disk, Wi (the Sun, a male god). Wi was placed above the Earth to give it heat and to make shadows for all things on it. When Maka asked for relief from the heat, Shkan commanded Wi to follow Anpao (dawn) across the sky. Thus, when Wi went below the Earth at night, Anpao followed. When Wi returned above the Earth in the morning, Anpao preceded it.

The rank of powers changed afterwards: Wi became first, Shkan, second, Maka, third and Inyan, having given away all his powers, ranked last. In the second stage of creation, the four superiors were given the power to be creators in turn and they created the four associates: Wi (the Sun) created Han-wi (the night-sun or goddess moon) to be his wife. Maka (the Earth) created Unk (passion), Shkan (the sky), himself a motion giver, created Tate (the wind), and Inyan (the stone god) created Wakinyan (the Great Thundering – the Winged One who controls lightning and storms). From these ancestor figures were created all the plants and animals and finally the people.

At the yearly Sun (or Thirst) Dance Festival of the prairie nations (e.g. Dakota and Plains Cree peoples), the sun was traditionally revered as the creator of light and heat. When a Sun Dance was held during the full moon, the dancers also gazed up at the moon, believing it to be the Master of Life for it could see all things, even when hidden underground.

Thus, in the beginning, everything was created by these great spiritual deities. Some Plains Cree emphasize that Thunder Bird is the key being in the Sun Dance, while others focus upon Buffalo. There was no object, however trivial, without its own wakan (spiritual life-force). Even sticks and clay had a spiritual essence which had to be revered; if they were not shown due respect, even these lowly spirits could vent their wrath upon the people. To this day when the pipe is smoked and passed around in the sweat lodge, people claim to be aware of the presence of the ancestral figures among them.

3. CREATION AND EMERGENCE[3]
An Apache creation story

It is dark in the underworld before the emergence. Dissatisfied, Holy Boy decides there should be light. He tries again and again to make the sun and the moon, using many different materials, but he is always unsuccessful. Whirlwind tells Holy Boy that White Hactcin (Spirit) and Black Hactcin have the sun and the moon. Holy Boy acquires the sun and the moon from them, and when the necessary songs and rituals are completed, they rise, bringing light to the underworld.

The many medicine people living in the underworld begin to argue fiercely, all claiming to have been responsible for bringing light. On the fourth day, the sun and the moon rise to the centre of the sky, and because the medicine people continue to argue all around them, they escape up through the hole in the centre of the sky, to emerge in the present Earth. Despite all their efforts the medicine people are unable to bring them back.

The Hactcin direct the medicine men to make an elaborate sand painting: a world bordered with four mountains, each symbolized by a pile of different coloured sand. Then the Hactcin choose twelve medicine people, and paint and costume six of them to represent summer and six to represent winter. Finally a further six are selected and dressed as clowns (they are painted white all over with black stripes).

As these people sing and dance, the mountains begin to grow, and when they have reached nearly to the sky, Fly and Spider are sent up to the world above. They bring back four rays of the sun from which the Hactcin construct a ladder of twelve steps. At first when the animals are sent up the ladder they report that the world above is covered with water. Then the Hactcin go up and prepare the Earth for the others to enter. The emergence proceeds from this point, with the clowns leading the way, laughing to scare off any sickness, then First Man and First Woman, followed by the twelve medicine people, and finally by all the animals and birds.

Once they have emerged, Changing Woman – one of the Holy People – teaches the mortals how to live in harmony with nature. She also builds the first hogan (house) out of turquoise and shell, and gives the gift of corn to the people.

Finally, two old people try to enter the world, but the ladders are now worn out and they cannot climb them. They call for help, but there is no way for them to emerge. The old people angrily proclaim they will remain in the underworld, to which all those who have emerged will one day have to return, thus designating the underworld as the place of death.

Among the many forces threatening the humans are the Hactcin or Holy

People themselves. These are strange and powerful spirit beings who travel on the wind, sunbeams, rainbows or lightning flashes. Though they have created the people, they are not always benign and demand frequent ritual acts and ceremonies lest they use their power to harm people. They frequently cause droughts, crop failure, sickness or other misfortunes. Even more fearsome are the Chinde, the ghosts of Earth Surface dead. Among the Holy People only Changing Woman is always benevolent.

*Navajo world-view, portrayed as a sand painting
(after Trudy Griffin-Pierce, University of Arizona)*

The *Dinétah* (sacred homeland) of the *Diné* (the people), as the Navajo call themselves, centres around the family hogan or house. The first house was built at the place where the ancestors emerged from the lower three worlds into this 'glittering' place. It is bounded by four sacred mountains: Blanca Peak (east), Mount Taylor (south), San Francisco Peaks (west) and Hesperus Peak (north). Each quarter of this creation is symbolized by its own colour, and sacred person. The fertility of the Earth is shown by symbols for corn. Above it is the dome of the sky filled with constellations and the Milky Way, and guarded by a rainbow god. At either side of the sky young warriors hold up the sun and the moon, while beyond the sky is the realm ruled by Big Wind (left) and Big Thunder (right).

Early in the twentieth century, the great Navajo Hatali, or medicine man, Hosteen Klah recounted a story of how the stars got into the sky:

> First Woman decided to spell out all the laws needed by the First People. Laws could not be written in sand or on water, since few people would see them before they disappeared. But when the laws were written in the sky, everyone could look up and study them. First Man and First Woman had all the stars laid out on a blanket and were setting each star in place when the trickster Coyote came along. Coyote wanted to help, but the work of placing and naming the stars was too slow for him. So he grabbed a corner of the blanket and flipped the remaining stars into the sky.
>
> (Carlson and Sacha, p. 103)

4. THE ORIGINS OF GOOD AND EVIL
An Iroquois creation story

To the Six Nations of the Iroquois and to the Hurons, the world in which they lived was one where the forces of good and evil were inherent in all of nature. They perceived that this had always been so since the beginning.

Their world was full of invisible spirits, whose earthly symbols could be seen everywhere. Some of these were False Faces, demon-like spirits that could cause disease. Fortunately, their great powers could also be harnessed or actually reversed. The men who were initiated into the False Face Society manipulated the forces of the supernatural, and used the very forces that had caused the sickness to effect its cure.

Human life began when Sky Woman was pushed out of heaven. Two loons caught her on their wings and carried her down. However, the world was covered with water and the only place to place her was upon the back of Turtle. Various animals were asked to dive down and bring up some earth. Beaver, Muskrat and Diver all failed, but at last Toad returned with some earth in his mouth and placed it on a Turtle's shell. As Turtle grew, so also did the land, to form an enormous fertile island for Sky Woman to live on.

She had already become pregnant by Earth Holder before she was pushed out of heaven, and once on Turtle Island she gave birth to twins, two sons who had very different dispositions, Great Spirit and Evil Spirit. The children began to fight even before they were born, but in giving birth to the second child – Evil Spirit – Sky Mother died.

Great Spirit saw that although Sky Mother was dead, her influence would remain. She was buried in the earth. From her head he fashioned the sun; from her body, the moon and stars. Not content with this work, Great Spirit turned his attention to the Earth resting upon the turtle shell, and he made the seas, the rivers, the mountains and valleys, and finally people, and animals. From Sky Mother's body grew plants like pumpkin and beans and corn, that the people needed to live.

Evil Spirit worked too, and from his labours came contention, strife, anger and warfare, as well as creatures dangerous to all other living things.

Obviously, two such opposite spirits could not live together, and so Great Spirit and Evil Spirit fought for two whole days. Evil Spirit was defeated and forced into exile in the netherworld, but his handiwork remained behind to bedevil the children of the Earth.

5. THE RAVEN, THE FIRST PEOPLE AND THE LIGHT
A Haida-Gwai story from the west coast of Canada

Bill Reid's monumental carving in Yellow Cedar of 'The Raven and the First Men' stands as a great centrepiece in the Museum of Anthropology, at the University of British Columbia, Vancouver, and is often regarded as one of the holiest places in Canada. Bill Reid (1920–), Haida jeweller and carver, and one of Canada's greatest artists, has successfully used the complex principles of Haida two-dimensional design to communicate emotions such as awe and passion. He is able to take the mythological figure of Raven, and communicate to today's world something of the mystery, magic and holiness of creation.

Before there was anything, a great flood covered the Earth. After the flood receded it left a great stretch of mud, and in the mud Raven found a giant clam shell. When he looked closely he saw that the clam shell was full of little tiny creatures that looked very timid and afraid.

Raven spoke to them gently and coaxed them to come out, but soon grew tired of these silly little two-legged creatures that were so timid and had neither feathers nor beaks. Growing on the rocks were red chitons, and Raven mated the

Raven and the creation of man

chitons with these little creatures. Eventually there were born to the chitons a race of brown-skinned, black-haired humans. These children were no longer timid shell-dwellers, but beautiful strong people, who grew up and built fine lodges along the shores and decorated them with heraldic carvings that told of the legendary beginnings of their families.

Raven is sometimes called the great transformer, for he not only released the first people from the clam shell but also, when all the world was pitch black, he stole the light from an old man who had all the light of the universe stored in the central and smallest of a set of nesting boxes. The old man lived in a cabin beside the river with his daughter, and he kept the light securely hidden in case his daughter was ugly.

By trickery and cunning Raven turned himself into a single hemlock needle floating on the water. When the daughter came and filled her basket with water and drank some, she swallowed Raven, who grew inside her and eventually was born as her child and, therefore, as the old man's grandson. As he grew the grandson begged and pleaded for the boxes to play with until, one at a time, he was given them all. When he received the smallest box that was filled with all the light of the universe, he turned himself back into a Raven and flew up the smoke-hole into the sky. He did not notice Eagle above him, and when Eagle swooped down upon him he dropped half of the light which shattered when it hit the Earth, the fragments making the moon and stars. Eagle pursued him over the rim of the Earth where he dropped the other piece to form the sun. The next morning, when the rays of the sun shone down the lodge smoke-hole, the old man finally saw that his daughter was beautiful – there had been no need to hide the light.

'Everything is in a circle'
(Black Elk)

3 | THE SACRED CIRCLE OF LIFE

Though First Nations Peoples represent a multitude of related cultures, with a great variety of mythology and of religious ceremonies, the universal starting point that all hold in common is that all of life is spiritual: everything that exists, animals, plants, people, rocks, the sun and stars have elements of sacredness.

The most frequent and fundamental symbol of all existence for the Plains Peoples is the symbol of the circle, often called the 'Medicine Wheel'. Thus the primary metaphor of existence, the circle, is both a spatial metaphor and an inclusive metaphor. Creation itself is viewed not from a linear or historical perspective but from within cyclical thinking. This is evident in nearly all aspects of existence, in ceremonial structures, symbols, architecture, and in the symbolic parameter of the community's universe. Listen to the words of Black Elk:

> You have noticed that everything an Indian does is in a circle, and that is because the Power of the World always works in circles, and everything tries to be round.
>
> In the old days when we were strong and happy people, all our power came to us from the sacred hoop of the nation, and as long as the hoop was unbroken, the people flourished. The flowering tree was the centre of the hoop, and the circle of the four quarters nourished it. The East gave peace and light, the South gave warmth, the West gave rain, and the North with its cold

and mighty wind gave us strength and endurance. This knowledge came to us from the outer world with our religion.

Everything the Power of the World does is done in a circle. The sky is round, and I have heard that the earth is round like a ball, and so are all the stars. The wind, in the greatest power, whirls. Birds make their nests in circles, for theirs is the same religion as ours. The sun comes forth and goes down again in a circle. The moon does the same, and both are round. Even the seasons form a great circle in their changing, and always come back again to where they were. The life of a man is a circle from childhood to childhood, and so it is in everything where power moves. Our teepees were round like the nests of birds, and these were always set in a circle, the nation's hoop, and nest of many nests, where the Great Spirit meant for us to hatch our children.
(*Black Elk Speaks*, p. 194)

THE SPATIAL METAPHOR OF THE SACRED HOOP

The existence of First Nations Peoples is deeply rooted in the land, for without the land that sustains them, people cannot live. The varied patterns of economic activity and the related and equally varied cultures of First Nations Peoples depend upon the characteristics and potential of the land.

Northern groups in the arctic and taiga forests generally follow a seasonal migration pattern, fishing and sealing in the Arctic waters, and following the caribou herds in their annual migration across the Arctic plains. In the forested and abundant west coast regions, hunting and berry picking supplement fishing. Here, many communities have winter villages with substantial family and community lodges, and also temporary summer quarters where they move at the time of salmon migration to harvest and dry fish. In the dry south-west of America, in the semi-desert and high plateau regions, corn is a basic staple, and is grown together with beans, squash, potatoes and numerous other garden crops. Here people are particularly dependent upon rainfall, and many of their religious rites and prayers are related to rain and to the growth of corn. In the central plains the buffalo herds once provided the basic support for the life of the people, supplying them not only with food, but also with materials for clothing, shelter and weapons. Today the buffalo herds have been eliminated by the settlers, and totally new ways of life had to be established. In the forested eastern regions of both Canada and USA, the basic activities of hunting were supplemented by harvesting natural products such as wild rice, maple sugar, and berries and by cultivating gardens.

> The life of people became a reflection of the life of the earth and our ancestors became intimately connected and inseparable from these realities. Through many years of experience, trial and error, hunger and hardship, our ancestors learned that the depletion of plant and animal life in their immediate environment meant starvation and death.
> (Clarkson, Morrissette and Regallet, p. 10)

That the circle or 'Sacred Hoop' (the almost universal symbol of existence for First Nations Peoples) is spatial helps to explain the fact that Native spirituality and Native existence itself is deeply and inseparably rooted in the land. A people's culture and self-image is based upon the continuous habitation of a place. People and place together form a cultural unity. To understand this is to see why the conquest and removal of people from their traditional lands was effectively cultural genocide.

George Tinker, a Native theologian from Colorado, explains that:

> Native American spirituality and values, social and political structures, and even ethics are rooted not in some temporal notion of history but in spatiality. This is perhaps the most dramatic (and largely unnoticed) cultural difference between Native American thought and Western intellectual tradition.
>
> The question is not whether time or space is missing in one culture or the other, but which is dominant. Of course Native Americans have a temporal awareness, but it is subordinate to our sense of place. Likewise, the Western tradition has a spatial awareness, but it lacks the priority of the temporal. Hence, progress, history, development, evolution and process become key notions that invade all academic discourse in the West.
> (Tinker, pp. 15–16)

In its form as a medicine wheel, with two lines forming a cross drawn across it, the circle can symbolize the four directions of the Earth. Prayers can be addressed to the four directions and blessings sought from the different manifestations of the Spirit that are symbolized by these four directions.

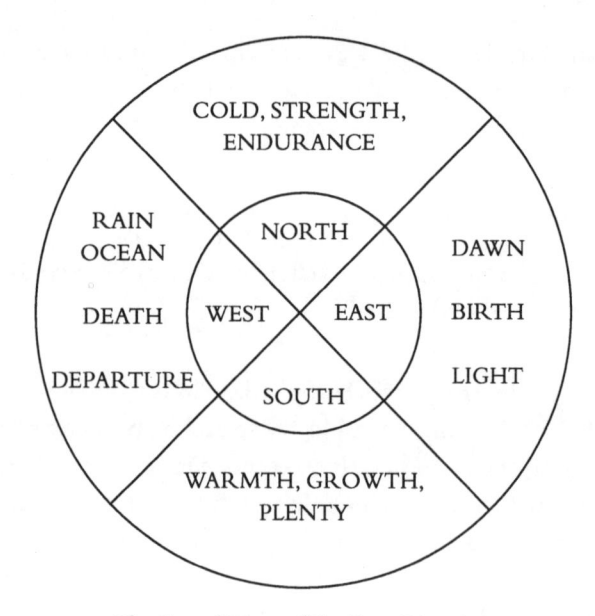

The Sacred Hoop of the Four Directions

The four directions can be associated with the four cardinal points (east, south, west and north), with any four sacred animals that have special and symbolic importance for a particular community, with four colours (frequently red, yellow, black and white), and with the four seasons and the blessings that each bring,

> Our ancestors tell us that the cycles of the seasons were in themselves full of meaning. The changing of the seasons reflected and paralleled the changes in our lives from birth to old age. Spring was a time of renewal, of new life and new beginnings, as in the birth of a child. Summer was a time of plenty, a time to explore and grow, as in the time of youth. Fall was the time to incorporate the teaching of the previous two cycles and to harvest and crystalize the knowledge that we had been given, as in the middle years of life. Winter was the time of patience and understanding and the time to teach and plan for the next cycle of life, the time of old age.
>
> (Clarkson, Morrissette and Regallet, p. 3)

The east symbolizes the dawn, creation, the coming of light and the new day. It may also represent spring and new life. Houses, lodges, hogans and sweat lodges are constructed so that the door opens to the east to let in dawn, spring, light and new life. South symbolizes summer, warm winds and rain, the growing season and bounty. West symbolizes the ocean, sunset, old age and death, the departure of the spirit. North symbolized winter and the cold, snow, strength, fireside story-telling.

A Prayer of the Four Directions

O Great Spirit of the East, and of the rising sun,
You are the Spirit of new life and new beginnings.
We pray that you will give us light, energy and power,
flooding our lives with illumination and understanding,
and blessing us with the vision of the sacredness of creation.

O Great Spirit of the South, of all green and growing things,
You are the Spirit of warm summer rains, and gentleness.
We pray that your warm winds will warm our hearts.
Bring to the land abundance and let everything
rejoice and grow and be fruitful.

O Great Spirit of the West, and of the sunset,
You are the Spirit of the great waters and oceans.
We pray that your restless, shining waters
may cleanse and heal us, may refresh and strengthen us,
dissolving all barriers and bringing peace.

O Great Spirit of the North, and of the vast northern sky,
You are the Spirit of energy, the source of knowledge and wisdom.
We pray that your icy breath will sweep away the old patterns,
that your cold sharpness will awaken our spirits, clear our minds,
and give us wisdom and clear vision for the future.

THE INCLUSIVE METAPHOR OF THE SACRED HOOP

The fundamental symbol of all existence, the circle, is also a symbol signifying the family, the clan, the tribe or nation, and eventually all of creation. Every person, from the youngest new-born child to the most respected of the elders, was an important part of the 'Sacred Hoop'. Because a circle has no beginning and no end, all parts of the circle are of equal value, and all have their own roles and parts to play, appropriate to their age and ability, if the circle is to be whole, healthy and unbroken.

First Nations Faith and Ecology

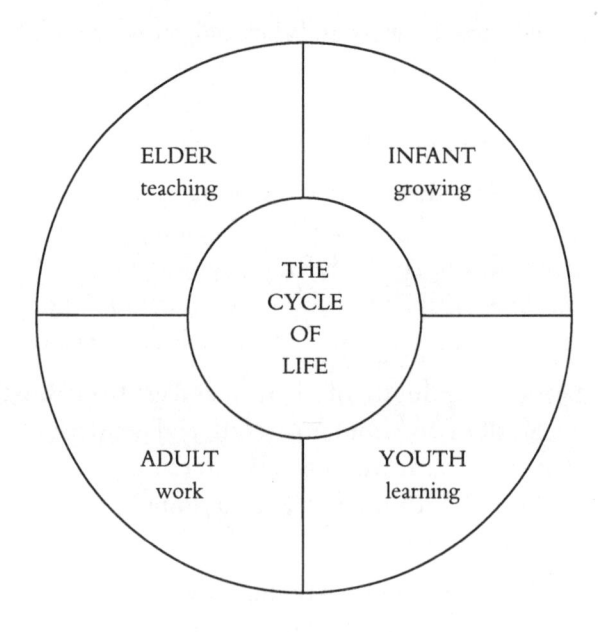

```
           ELDER         INFANT
          teaching       growing

                  THE
                 CYCLE
                  OF
                 LIFE

           ADULT          YOUTH
            work         learning
```

The Sacred Hoop of Life

A person's roles change through the different stages of life. Thus, a child's task is to grow and learn the basic skills needed to survive, and their responsibilities in the community. After coming of age, men and women are expected to take their place as mature members of the community: providing food, shelter, clothing and defence for the clan, caring for the young, old and sick, participating in religious traditions, etc. The elders of the community are revered for their experience and wisdom, and not only assist with the training and teaching of the young, but with the debates in decision-making assemblies. Thus individual lives are also seen as a circle, going from infant, to youth, to maturity and old age.

People cannot live for long in isolation from the community. Many tasks, including hunting, cultivating, building lodges and sea-going canoes are communal tasks.

> The development of Indigenous culture evolved inside the nation, band, community and the clan structure. This led to a sense of responsibility, that was actualized into a division of labour aimed at the benefit of the group. Each individual's activity with respect to survival was only one aspect of meeting

The sacred circle of life

the needs of the group. All members were expected to contribute to the benefit of the larger group and no one person held a role any less significant than any other. This interdependence was again a reflection of the lessons of nature gleaned from the observation of the relationship of all living things to each other. In this relationship there was not only equality with the other spirits of the creation, but there was equality with all other people. No person was any less than the other, each had a role to perform in Creation by virtue of the gifts bestowed upon that person. Each person was quite simply only a piece of the overall scheme of things and had something to contribute that was valued equally with all others.

(Clarkson, Morrissette and Regallet, p. 13)

An individual's personal needs had to be balanced with those of the family, clan and tribe or nation. The self, family, clan and nation could be perceived as four directions of a circle which has to be kept in balance.

Connectedness and responsibility extended not only to the clan and group living at the present time, but included both past and future generations. The ancestors who had passed down to the group their wisdom and knowledge, and whose spirits might still be present, required respect. This was commonly put into practice by making offerings of tobacco and food, and in council meetings the spirit of the ancestors may be invoked, and their wisdom sought. Responsibility also extended to the yet unborn. Everything that was done was perceived as having consequences for later generations, and each generation had a responsibility to ensure survival for the seventh generation.

In traditional society all members participated in the daily work of economic survival and child-raising. In addition were tasks specifically belonging to a clan or age group. In the following diagram it can be seen that people play more than one role. At certain seasons the majority of people are all needed to hunt or fish or plant and harvest. Much of work and economic production was communal, and all were expected to contribute to the well-being of the community as a whole. These economic activities do not free people from their religious, social or political responsibilities, but are intimately linked with them, for each person is part of the community as a whole, and each person's welfare is bound up with the well-being and proper functioning of the community as a whole. But the welfare of the community is also intimately bound up and dependent upon the well-being of the greater society – Creation.

The Sacred Hoop of the Nation, showing those responsible for various tasks

When Cree Elder Stan McKay speaks of 'all my family', he means not only his wife and children, aunts, uncles, cousins, and grandparents but the entire Sacred Hoop of 'the two and four legged, the winged and the finned and the rooted ones' that form part of the great interdependent web of life. We may call the Earth 'our Mother' and the animals 'our brothers and sisters'. Even things that biologists describe as inanimate, we call our relatives. This calling of creation into our family is more than imagery, it describes a relationship of love and faithfulness between human persons and creation.

Whereas the mainstream view is that people and the environment are separate – the Earth consisting of resources which exist for people to use and exploit – the Native view is that people, the land, water, plants and animals form one unified and interdependent living system.

As all the points that make up the circle are connected, so is every aspect of life. The sacred is not separate from the everyday world in which we live and work, but infuses everything. Therefore, every act, whether hunting or cultivating, caring for children and the sick, building a lodge, or looking after a fire, is a sacred act. This is very different from Western society where religion is kept for one day of the week, and prayer belongs in churches or temples. In traditional society, prayers, and sacred rites accompanied every aspect of life. The hunter would not kill, nor the cultivator plant, children would not be named, nor the sick healed without appropriate sacred prayers and rites.

Everything – spiritual, human and natural – has its place in the cycle of life, and interference with any component, no matter how small, will eventually have repercussions on all the other components. Listen to the words of Bella T'seleie in 1990:

> Everything in this world is interconnected and it won't be long before all these problems (pollution) start affecting us. It's when we start trying to change the environment and try to wipe out certain species, even something as small as the mosquito, that we begin to break down the environment.

THE EARTH IS NOT PROPERTY

This view of respect for the sacredness of Mother Earth, means that the Earth cannot be viewed as a commodity to be bought and sold. Nor does it exist solely for the use of humans. All of life has access rights to the use of the land and its gifts within reason. While people had to respect the rights of prior users and of the hunting territories of other families and nations, and permission might be sought to use a given piece of land, the limit of use was the reality that exploiting the land to extinction would ultimately mean your own extinction. As Oren Lyons (1984) stated:

> We Native people did not have the concept of private property in our lexicon, and the principles of private property were pretty much in conflict with our value system. For example you wouldn't see 'No hunting' or 'No fishing' or 'No trespassing' signs in our territories. To a Native person such signs would have been equivalent to 'no breathing' because the air is somebody's private property. If you said to the people, 'the Ontario Government owns all the air in Ontario, and if you want some, you are going to have to go and see the Bureau of Air', we would all laugh.

The land is where our ancestors are buried. The land is the birthright and only possible means of sustenance for our children. Each of us has, therefore, a great responsibility to protect and care for it. People are placed on the earth (our Mother) to be the caretakers of all that is here, not to exploit or destroy or sell it.

RESPONSIBILITY TO THE SEVENTH GENERATION

Many of the decisions that are made today by corporations and by our governments take a very short-term view. Governments frequently develop five-year plans, while corporations generally seek only to make an immediate profit. This short-sighted approach has meant that, as governments change and corporations merge or move, there is no accountability when the negative effects of industrialization policies become apparent many years or even decades later.

When Native Bands consider development options, they consider what the likely impacts will be, not only in the immediate future, but upon their children and children's children to the seventh generation. They want a cleaner, non-exploitative and healthier world for future generations.

In 1983 the respected Ojibway Elder Art Solomon wrote the following prayer:

> Grandfather, look at our brokenness.
>
> Now we must put the sanctity of life
> as the most sacred principle of power,
> and renounce the awesome might of materialism.
>
> We know that in creation, only the family of man
> has strayed from the sacred way.
>
> We know that we are the ones who are divided
> and we are the ones who must come back together,
> to worship and walk in a sacred way,
> that by our affirmation we may heal the Earth and heal each other.
>
> Now we must affirm life for all that is living
> or face death in a final desecration with no reprieve.

We hear the screams of those who die for want of food,
and whose humanity is aborted and prevented.

Grandfather, the sacred one,
we know that unless we love and have compassion
the healing cannot come.

Grandfather, teach us how to heal our brokenness.

MONDAMIN

In the time of the beginning a young boy lived with his grandmother Mondamin. She raised him and cared for him until he grew up to be a strong and courageous young hunter.

Every planting season Mondamin planted her garden of beans, squash and herbs. Then the rains came, the garden grew, and in the harvest season, she gathered the ripe produce.

But one year, when the planting season came, and she planted out her garden, no rains came. Every dawn she would wake and after giving thanksgiving, would scan the sky, searching for signs of rain clouds. The shamans and the people had enacted the proper rituals, the sacred chants had been chanted, yet somehow they must have offended the kachina spirits, for no rain came. In the garden, the young plants had withered and died, while in the hills, the animals had moved far away searching for streams. Day after day the hunters journeyed further, but always came back with nothing. And the people grew very hungry.

Eventually, Mondamin looked in her storage pots, and they were empty. There was nothing left to eat. She called her grandson and said to him: 'This is what you must do. Take your hunting knife and kill me, and then bury my body in the garden.'

At first the grandson refused, saying: 'Only wait a few more days grandmother, I will hunt once more, and surely I will return with some game for the pot, and all will be well.'

Early every morning he set out for the hills to hunt, and every evening he returned empty handed. And the people grew very weak with hunger.

Again Mondamin called her grandson. Again she told him to kill her and bury her body in the garden. At last, and with a heavy heart, the young hunter did as Mondamin asked. As he placed her body in the ground his tears watered the earth. Worn out from hunger, exhaustion and grief, he slept.

When he awoke and went out to mourn where he had buried Mondamin, a beautiful maiden had sprung up from the ground. Her slender body was clad in deep green, and silky, tasselled hair fell softly around her yellow face. She greeted the grandson with joy.

'Every year you must do this', she said. 'Plant my body in the soil each growing season, and gather my ripe heads of corn (maize) each harvest season. Dry and store my grain in your storage jars and you will never hunger again.'

TEACHINGS OF THE TEPEE

The tepee is a familiar sight to the First Nations of the Central Plains of North America such as the Sioux, Blackfoot and Cree. There, at almost all pow-wows, Native gatherings and public events, as well as at religious ceremonies, tepees will be erected. Frequently a sacred fire will be carefully tended and kept burning in the centre of the tepee, so that the smoke can rise up through the central vent. People may enter and sit in a circle around the edge for prayer and meditation or to listen to spiritual teaching of the elders. Each part of the tepee is charged with meaning and symbolism, and the elders may relate their teachings of values to various parts of the tepee.

The poles represent:
1. Obedience.
2. Respect.
3. Humility.
4. Happiness.
5. Love.
6. Faith.
7. Kinship.
8. Cleanliness.
9. Thankfulness.
10. Sharing.
11. Strength.
12. Good child-raising.
13. Hope.
14. Ultimate protection.
15. Controls flaps from wind.

The sacred circle of life

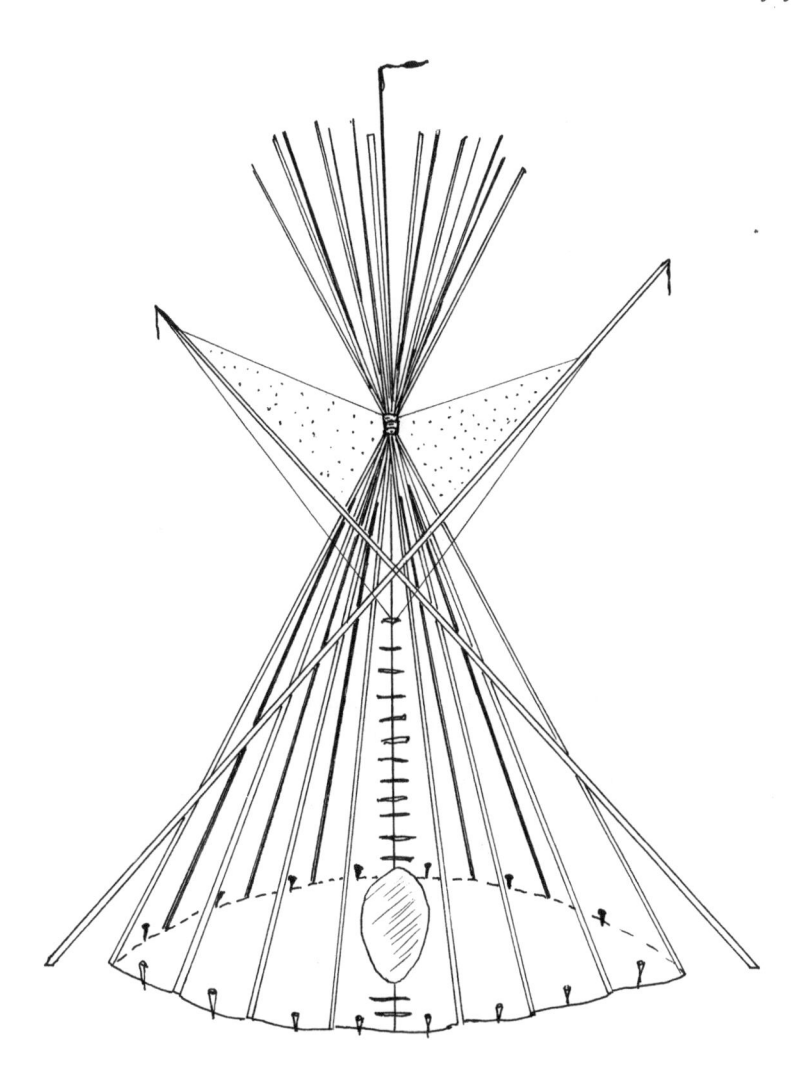

The thong binding the poles – relationship.
The fourteen pins closing the tent – keeping the family intact.
The hide (or canvas) covering – warmth and protection.
The pegs that anchor the tent – fasting and self-discipline.

Lillooet people's story about the killing of a bear:

*'You died first, greatest of all animals.
We respect you, and will treat you accordingly'*

4 | ANIMALS ARE SACRED

Spirituality is seen as a pervasive dimension of all life and, therefore, all animals are a part of a sacred Creation and contain a spirit essence no less significant than our own. Each creature is placed on Earth to fulfil a purpose that is intimately connected to all other beings, and environmental events may be influenced by spiritual forces. Above all, humans do not have any special superiority or authority over other life-forms. All creatures, and all parts of creation contain a spiritual dimension and must, like people, be treated with respect.

RESPECT

Nature is viewed as 'hierophanic', or as a source of spiritual revelation. All of nature, but especially certain creatures such as the eagle, raven, buffalo, owl, salmon and many others, are to be treated with reverence. Not only animals, but rivers, mountains or mesas and other sites may be regarded as sacred, because in their presence one becomes aware of the simplicity and mystery of life. Such creatures and places become manifestations of spiritual reality. Nature itself is the cathedral, the site where the spiritual may be encountered.

In Ojibwa belief, hunting success and spiritual powers are closely associated. Human, natural and spiritual worlds are tightly interwoven, and hunters may offer prayers before a mountain or before a lake, asking for the blessing of good weather, good crops and successful hunting. There is a reciprocity between the human and spiritual world based on gift and gratitude, which may be expressed with offerings or dances.

Wild animals must be respected and should be left alone – they should not be held in captivity and humans should not interfere with their natural habitat or behaviour. A story is often recounted of the first priest to come north to Fort Good Hope. Despite warnings, he captured a live caribou and used it as a dog to pull his sled. He fenced an area to keep it in, but one morning he went out to check on the caribou and it was gone. The story ends with these words of warning:

> Since that time the caribou didn't migrate up this way for many years. Big game like that are wild. You can't treat them like dogs. That's why they didn't come back for many years. It left its old migration route.
> (Albert Lafferty, 1990, recorded by Johnson, p. 74)

The hunter may not take the life of an animal without making a reciprocal offering. Among many tribes the traditional offering is tobacco, or some other recognition of respect and acknowledgement of the hunter's reliance upon the Creator and upon the animal for survival. Humans and animals have a reciprocal relationship towards one another. Animals are available for human use, and humans in turn are expected to treat them with dignity and respect. In taking a life in the plant or animal world, we should enter into a relationship of great respect and humility, because the spirit is being asked to sacrifice itself so that other people can live. As marks of respect, different practices are followed. Among the west-coast Lillooet people, when a bear of any variety was killed, the hunters sang the bear-song – a mourning song. Singers often wept and prayed to the bear as they sang. Here are the words of one such song:

> You died first, greatest of animals.
> We respect you, and will treat you accordingly.
> (Recorded by Teit)

Traditions dictated that certain animals had to be carried whole to the camp before skinning or cutting. Hides and meat of certain animals

Animals are sacred

could only be used for certain purposes. For example it would be disrespectful to step over hides, or to give certain parts of the meat to dogs. Some parts of the animal contained special powers and might be kept and worn as charms to bring success in further hunting. When hunting big game, you have to respect the bones and hide. Some of the bones play important symbolic roles in rituals and ceremonies; for example, the buffalo skull is used in the Sun Dance and other ceremonies. Johnson records a Dene hunter from northern Canada as saying:

> When hunting big game, you have to respect the bones and hide, or they will never go back to that area again. . . . If you don't keep the law you'll have bad luck in hunting and trapping.

Similarly, people of the Pacific northwest coast traditionally returned the bones of salmon to the sea. A Squamish legend that begins: 'Long ago when animals and humans were the same . . .' continues to recount how the people of the west coast were hungry. So three brothers set out by canoe and eventually came to the home of the salmon people. Some of the young salmon people were ordered by their chief to enter the water where they became salmon. They were caught and satisfied the hunger of the three guests, and as soon as the bones were collected and returned to the sea, they turned back into salmon people again. The Salmon Chief promised that every year he would send first the spring salmon, then the sockeye, followed by the cohoe, the dog-salmon and lastly the humpback, as long as they returned the bones to the ocean to return to their home across the water towards the rising sun, so that the salmon people could live to return again the following year (Clark, pp. 29–32). There are variations in this story among the coastal people. See page 38 for how it is told by the Haida.

Many hunting traditions are not only respectful, but also describe very sound methods of conservation:

1. It is understood by all that you 'take only what you need, and you leave the rest'. If you kill more than is needed, or waste part of the kill, then the animal spirits will be offended and will disappear from the area, making future hunting impossible. One important principle was common to all First Nations Peoples – they did not take more than they needed.
2. Another common practice is to hunt only mature animals, and

SALMON BOY
A Salish and Haida – west-coast myth

Long ago there lived a young boy who would not show respect for the salmon, although the life and well-being of the north-west Coast peoples depended upon the annual salmon migration. When the people eat salmon they give thanks to them and return their bones to the water, to ensure the Salmon People can come back to life and return the following year. But this young boy just carelessly threw the bones and scraps away on the ground. This angered the Salmon People and later, when he went swimming, the current caught him and swept him away to the bottom of the river.

The spirits of the Salmon People, who had left their bodies behind for the human and animal people to use as food, took the boy with them back to the ocean where they lived throughout the winter, and when they returned to the river in the spring, he swam with them, for he had become one of the Salmon People. As they passed his village, his own mother caught him and recognized the copper necklace that he was wearing. Salmon Boy remained with his people throughout the summer, teaching them many things. As he requested, the village people placed him back in the river in the fall, where his body died and his soul returned to the ocean with the Salmon People.

In another version of this important myth it is a brother and sister who dwell in the ocean with the Salmon People and return to their village each year.

In the summer of 1994 the renowned Salish sculptor Roy Henry Vickers unveiled a 30-foot-high totem pole that he had carved for Saanich Commonwealth Place, the aquatic centre for the Commonwealth Games in Victoria. Carved from a single cedar from Walbran Valley on Vancouver Island, he carved the pole to depict the brother and sister, who magically lead the salmon back each year to the Salish in an eternal cycle of renewal. This modern totem stands as both a hymn to the natural world and as a warning of what we could easily lose if we do not respect nature.

never to kill the females when they are pregnant or caring for their young. A Dene (northern) hunter reported:

> Even long ago when the hunters opened up the lodges, if they caught a small beaver, they would let it go. We usually hunted the older ones, and the two and three year olds. And the young ones were left alone. In the spring time the mother is not hunted because they usually have kids then.
> (Gabe Kochon, 1990, recorded by Johnson, p. 75)

3. Hunters believe that when a species becomes scarce then the area should be rested for a period of time to allow the population to renew itself. Hunters should move on to another area.
4. Respect is accorded not only to the animals hunted but also to the land.

> We depend on our land so much. It's just like our store. We worry about the oil companies really cleaning up after themselves like they say they do when they go on the lakes, like this last spring. The ice road the oil company made has a lot of diesel on it. This can't be good for the fish. We worry about things like that because we only have our land to depend on and what we get from it.
> (Richard Kochon, 1985, recorded by Johnson, p. 75)

THE HUNT

Hunting is essential to survival. It is not merely an economic activity, it is a holy occupation. Animals are seen as living in a way similar to people as regards feelings, emotions and the purpose of life, the major difference between them being only in outward form. Therefore, in many communities hunting has become a magico-religious activity, and various rites may be associated with different aspects of both locating animals and making the kill. Women frequently participate in hunting, in fishing, and in operating trap lines. In most communities can be found widows, even those extremely old, whose prowess in hunting is legendary.

Tanner (1979) commented that frequently animals are thought of, and spoken to, as if they had human personalities and entered into conversations and various relationships with the hunters. These relations are frequently elaborated in myths and legend, songs and story-telling. He notes three broad categories of such relationships:

1. The idealized relationship (some would say a love relationship) exists where the hunter pays respect to the animal, acknowledging its superior status, following which the animal then willingly 'gives itself' or sacrifices itself in an act of generosity to the hunter.
2. During the process of the hunt, the hunter perceives events from the perspective of the animal, entering, as it were, the animal's body. Numerous stories recount events alternating between the point of view of the hunter and of the hunted. People with this special ability of transforming themselves into the thinking and feeling of the animals are highly respected, and sometimes referred to as 'transformers'.
3. A relationship of control, where the hunter uses magic to compel the animal to approach. Shamans sometimes claim the power to be able to compel animals to allow themselves to be caught. Among some communities a 'shaking tent' ceremony is held. The 'shaking tent' is used for divination, to be able to see events, animals and people that are separated by great distances or by time, from those conducting the ceremony. It is sometimes used to locate a missing hunting party. Inside the shaking tent the spirit of an animal, for example a bear, is called up. Then a battle takes place between the spirit of the bear and the spirit of the shaman. If the bear is defeated the hunters anticipate being able to kill numerous bears in the next season.

Some groups, especially among the Algonkian Peoples, have stories and legends that perceive animals as pursuing a social existence similar to that of people, in which an animal spirit becomes the 'Animal Master' (or Boss) of the species. Thus, before hunting, offerings of tobacco and petitions for success need to be addressed to the Animal Master who controls the species and thus determines the success or failure of the hunt.

GUARDIAN SPIRITS – THE PROTECTION AND FRIENDSHIP OF ANIMALS

Many people experience a special relationship of privilege with a particular species such as the bear, raven, elk or beaver. In parts of northern and eastern Canada this close friendship is sometimes recorded in stories about hunters who have killed a large number of a particular species. It may be felt that the species favours him, or that he is the animal's 'friend'. On the hunter's death, this animal species may mourn for him, or, if it is very sad, may leave the area entirely. Occasionally a 'shaking tent' ceremony may be held. At this time the shaman will face to the west (the opposite direction to the usual), the direction of the sunset symbolizing departing souls. If the shaman sees the dead man travelling to the west being followed by his animal friends, then it is known that these animals will leave the area, and the group will not be able to hunt them for a long time.

A practice which was once almost universal, and is now seeing a revival, is that of young people making a vision quest. First, the one 'crying for a vision' seeks the guidance of a respected elder or spiritual teacher who will direct the ceremony. Offerings will be made, then the seeker will assist in building a purification or sweat lodge. Then will follow some days of fasting and concentration when, alone before nature, the quester hopes to see in visions or dreams beyond the physical world to the spiritual reality that underlies it. It is through purification, fasting and self-discipline, that experience of the spiritual realm is sought.

Sometimes during the vision quest an animal may approach, in actuality or in a dream, and bring a message. This animal will then become the seeker's guardian spirit. They may experience a very close relationship with this species for the rest of their lives, will entirely cease to hunt it and turn to it for help in times of stress. Stories abound of how guardian spirit animals have come to the assistance of their human friends who are in some kind of trouble, perhaps injured in a road accident or lost in the bush.

Individual people, families and clans may thus have guardian spirits. Among the West Coast Peoples, the raven was a frequent guardian spirit who brought prophetic gifts, especially the ability to foresee the weather or foretell a death. The seal was another common guardian spirit. The stronger guardian spirits for warriors were traditionally hawks and eagles. For hunters, the most powerful were buffalo, bear, wolf, lynx, deer and beaver. The most potent for shamans were ravens, the golden eagle, mink and owl.

The shaman, medicine man or woman, or 'healer', is generally believed to have a special relationship with the animal spirits, and to be able to converse with them. Their guardian animal spirit in particular may appear to them in dreams and visions to give either assistance or a warning. The shaman's main task is healing, and the well-being of the community, and he or she will often act as an intermediary between a petitioner or ill person and the animal spirit. For example, notice that in the Inuit story of Sedna (pages 81–2), it is Sedna, the keeper of the animals, who dwells at the bottom of the sea; and when animals become scarce, and people are hungry, it is the task of the shaman to enter the sea, at considerable risk to himself, to communicate with her and ask her to let the animals return.

For Plains people, Tatanka, the Buffalo Spirit, is very holy,

> he is the Indian's brother, the giver of health, food and life. We Sioux consider ourselves part of the Tatanka Oyate, the Buffalo Nation, so closely are we connected to this wonderful Supernatural. . . . The Buffalo Spirit is part of all our sacred rites. . . . Tob Tob, the Bear Spirit, is the wisest of all spirits. Tob Tob created the four-legged beings. He is Great Medicine, the Healer of Wounds who teaches medicine men the secret language of the shaman.
>
> (Laviolette, p. 257)

ANIMALS – MYTHOLOGICAL AND REAL

First Nations societies enjoyed a much deeper relationship with the animal world than modern societies do. Individuals and entire clans would have a special and very close relationship with a particular animal that would be regarded as their totem or guardian spirit. Members of the clan would not hunt or harm that particular species, but rather regard it as their guardian and adviser, who would also care for their descendants.

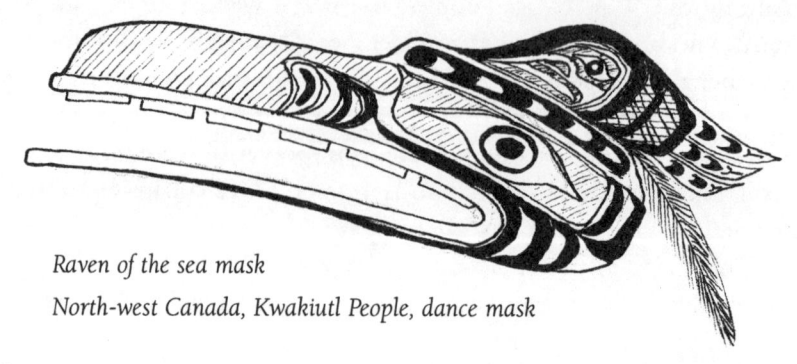

Raven of the sea mask
North-west Canada, Kwakiutl People, dance mask

On the west coast the history and ancestry of a clan, and its close relationship to certain animals, was depicted in beautifully carved totem poles. Thus a totem pole displaying a bear, a raven and a beaver is a form of mythical clan history and a proud assertion of lineage. Clan members are felt to be imbued with some of the qualities of their totem or guardian spirits. Magnificently carved, painted, and decorated sea-going canoes, houses, clothing and numerous household objects also depict stylized versions of animals who figure prominently in clan stories as protective or guardian spirits.

There is also a continuum of the spirit within the whole of creation. No sharp line is drawn between the spiritual and material worlds. To many people the mythological creatures such as the thunderbird or giant snake are just as real as a bear or an eagle, and each play their own distinctive roles in stories, myths and tales of origin. The beautifully carved clan dance masks from the northwestern coastal communities depict both actual animals such as the bear, beaver, whale and raven and also mythical animal spirits such as the thunderbird.

Whether from the west coast, or the eastern forests, or the Pueblo cultures of the south-western USA, the dancer putting on a sacred animal mask for a ritual is not simply dressing up as an animal, but is becoming the actual spirit of that animal. The dancer in an eagle mask is bodying forth the archetype of eagleness – the eternal archetype of the soaring bird, and is also using this as an entry point into the transcendent or spiritual realm.

In the Pueblo (Hopi, Zuni and Navajo) traditions the dead are believed to return as kachinas. The word 'kachina' comes from *ka* (to respect) and *china* (spirit). But the numerous and distinctive kachinas are not confined to spirits of human dead, but also of animals, stars and natural forces. Those wearing the kachina masks in ceremonial dances take on their powers. This means accepting a heavy responsibility, for to act unwisely or indiscreetly at this time would provoke the anger of the spirit, and imperil the community.

THE 'TRICKSTER'

In many histories and stories the role of 'trickster' is essential. For the Nez Percé and people of the western plateaux, Coyote plays tricks upon unsuspecting people, introducing evil powers and making people angry with each other. In many Cree tales it is Wisakedjak who leads the animals into mischief. He is the subject of many stories told for amusement in the winter months, but he also is the one who brought misfortune and dissension and caused the Creator to bring the great flood to cleanse the Earth of evil. Similar to Coyote and Wisakedjak are Nanabozho of the Chippewa and Ojibwa, Napi or Old Man of the Blackfeet, and Raven of the Pacific Coast.

> Napi made the sun and the world, animals and the first people. He created the first buffaloes and told the Indians to shoot them with the bows and arrows he had made. . . . Everywhere in the Rocky Mountains are places where Napi slept or walked or hunted. As a culture hero, he was much like Nanabozho; as a cruel prankster and trickster, he was much like Coyote.
>
> (Clark, p. 16)

Glooscap, the main character in many of the Micmac and Malecite stories from the Maritimes, appears only as a benefactor and as a human or superhuman being, never as an animal or trickster.

5 | THE BROKEN HOOP

> For the Grandfathers had shown me my people walking on the black road and how the nation's hoop would be broken and the flowering tree be withered . . .
>
> (*Black Elk Speaks*, p. 147)

BROKEN LAND

When Columbus first landed in the Americas it has been estimated that there were at least 100 million people, or about one-fifth of the human race living there. Almost immediately on contact the population began to decline due to warfare and, more seriously at the beginning, to exposure to European diseases such as influenza, diphtheria, smallpox, measles, tuberculosis, chicken pox and cholera, for which they had no immunity.

> By 1600, after some twenty waves of pestilence had swept through the Americas, less than a tenth of the original population remained. Perhaps 90 million had died. . . . It was the greatest mortality in history.
>
> (Wright, p. 14)

In the eastern United States, ever-increasing numbers of arriving immigrants surged westwards, flowing over Native traditional hunting grounds and gardens. Having learned survival skills and been introduced to many things, from canoes and snowshoes, to tobacco and cultivated plants such as corn, pumpkin and squash, the settlers now surveyed and divided up the land into private ownership plots. Land became a commodity to be bought and sold. The Earth became a resource – a land for the taking – a virgin land to be conquered, controlled and made to yield up its resources. And in the way were the last remnants of the Indigenous population.

Many communities suffered armed attack, first by those who came to seek gold and to pillage, and later by streams of land-hungry European settlers with superior numbers and weapons, who perceived the land as virgin and empty – a continent free for the taking – and its original inhabitants little more than an insignificant nuisance to be cleared out of the way. Some groups, such as the Beothuk of Newfoundland, were totally eliminated by genocide, together with their wealth of experience, language, culture, beliefs and heritage.

'During early colonialism, infested blankets were used to wipe out entire Tribes and Nations of the Original Peoples of this land. . . . Sometimes it was intentional, other times not' (Robinson and Quinney, p. xix). Even as late as 1880 the deliberate dispatch of a cartload of blankets infested with smallpox to the Blackfoot Indians was recorded in southern Alberta.

In 1830 President Jackson signed into law a bill requiring all 'Indians' living east of the Mississippi to leave their homes and be relocated far to the west. Although Cherokee elders fought this policy in the federal courts for many years, the courts refused to recognize Native People's rights to their ancestral lands. Guarded by federal soldiers and attacked by bandits and thieves, many died of exhaustion, sickness and starvation along the 'Trail of Tears', before reaching an alien environment in the west.

Systematically areas of Treaty 'Reserve' land were seized or reduced in size. Black Elk commented on the fate of the Black Hills Lakota People in 1889:

> There was hunger among my people . . . because the Wasichus (settlers) did not give us all the food they promised in the Black Hills Treaty. They made the treaty themselves: our people did not want it and did not make it. They the Wasichus who made it had given us less than half as much as they promised. . . . The Wasichus had slaughtered all the bison and shut us up in pens . . . and now they had made another treaty to take away from us about half the land we had left.
>
> (*Black Elk Speaks*, p. 230)

Their removal cleared the way for the land to be surveyed and divided between railroad companies and settlers. Prairie grasses, passenger pigeons, buffalo, First Nations Peoples, all were swept aside in the settlers' mad greed to claim 'free' land, and to plough and 'break' the 'virgin' prairies. Following the slaughter of Lakota people at Wounded Knee, Black Elk recalled:

> there was a big blizzard, and it grew very cold. The snow drifted deep in the gulch, and it was one long grave of butchered women and children and babies, who had never done any harm and were only trying to run away.
>
> (*Ibid.*, p. 262)
>
> I did not know then how much was ended. When I look back now from this high hill of my old age, I can still see the butchered women and children lying heaped and scattered all along the crooked gulch as plain as when I saw them with eyes still young. And I can see that something else died there in the bloody mud, and was buried in the blizzard. A people's dream died there. It was a beautiful dream.
>
> (*Ibid.*, p. 270)

BROKEN COMMUNITIES

> After the 19th-century Indian wars had ended, the US government, eager to relieve itself of the burden of caring for the recently subdued tribes, turned towards a policy of forced assimilation. This policy found its chief expression in the Dawes General Allotment Act of 1887, which sought to break up the tribal lands and transform the Indians into the rough equivalent of white yeomen farmers on individually owned 160-acre plots, all 'surplus' lands would be available for sale to the whites. The results at this wholesale attempt at assimilation were disastrous for the Indians – 86 million reservation acres were lost, 90,000 Indians left homeless. . . . By the 1920s the Indian population of the United States had shrunk to approximately 245,000 – a battered, demoralized remnant riddled with poverty and disease. Those who had been forced into missionary- or government-run boarding schools were fitted for neither the tribal nor the white world. Many found their only solace in alcohol.
>
> (R.D., p. 392)

Despite the efforts of John Collier, USA Commissioner of Indian Affairs from 1933 to 1946, who managed to halt land allotments to settlers, improved educational and health facilities, and laid the basis for the Wheeler-Howard Act that returned to them the rights to practise their traditional religions, engage in economic development and form corporations, the situation did not materially improve. The end of the Second World War saw a continuous erosion of First Nations

First Nations Faith and Ecology

autonomy in the USA. The most drastic policy change was embodied in Concurrent Resolution 108, adopted in 1953, that sought the total assimilation of the Native population, with the progressive 'termination' of US Federal Government responsibility for reserve lands, and for adherence to the terms of treaties.

Listen to a part of the testimony of Earl Old Person (Blackfoot) objecting to the proposed Congressional legislation of 1966:

> In the past 190 years, the US Government has tried every possible way to get rid of the troublesome Indian problem he feels he has on his hands. First the Government tried extinction through destruction – where money was paid for the scalps of every dead Indian. Then the Government tried mass relocation and containment through concentration – the moving of entire tribes or parts of tribes to isolated parts of the country where they were herded like animals and fed like animals for the most part. Then the Government tried assimilation – where the reservations were broken up into allotments (an ownership system the Indians did not understand) and Indians were forced to try to live like 'white men'. Indian dances and Indian hand work was forbidden. A family's ration of food was cut off if anyone in the family was caught singing Indian songs or doing Indian hand craft. Children were physically beaten if they were caught speaking Indian languages. The termination was tried by issuing false patents in fee to Indian land owners – land was taken out of the trust relationship with the US Government and an unrestricted patent in fee was issued to the Indian whether he wanted it or not or whether he understood what was going on or not.
>
> None of these policies worked. They only seemed to make the Indians more determined than ever to keep their Indian ways and their Indian identity.
>
> (Earl Old Person)

In Canada, the situation was much the same:

> In the 1600s the British Government entered into an agreement with the Mohawk Nations of Canada. This agreement, documented on a beaded belt, is known as the 'Two-row Wampum'. The treaty recognizes the fact that the Mohawk First Nations and the English people are two distinct societies travelling along the river of life, each in their own canoe or boat. The two nations have their own systems of government, their own traditions and customs, their own spirituality, and their own laws. Each will respect the ways of the other and not impose its laws or ways upon the other. The two boats will never meet, but rather will travel side by side in harmony with each other.
>
> This treaty sums up the essence of sovereignty: the basic right of a people to be recognized as a distinct society as the first inhabitants of the land in which the Creator placed them, with the right to control their own affairs and destiny. This is a principle which all indigenous understand and which they see as absolutely necessary if they are to assume their full and rightful role in society.
>
> (Jacobs)

However,

> European encroachment and annexation of Indian land ensured that Indian communities were without a sufficient land base. This situation also meant that Native peoples had no economic base. Even more crucial is the fact that the loss of land entails the loss of the spirituality of a people. For Native people the relationship to the land is so intimately connected with one's relationship to the Creator that to lose one's land is to lose one's soul.
>
> (Jacobs)

With the loss of an adequate land resource base, and removal to the very small and usually resource-poor areas of the reserve lands, the destruction of an entire culture and way of life was assumed to be just a matter of time.

> The land is the closest tie to the Creator for it is our lands from which we began. It is our responsibility to care for Mother Earth, not to damage it or neglect our responsibility. The European way is one of destruction with mining, testing of bombs, and oil drilling, digging into the flesh of our Mother. To neglect and lose our land by the Loss of our Treaties through Canada's Constitution, will be to kill our Mother and break our deepest and strongest ties with the Creator. Our Spirituality will be broken instead of being used as the basis of our lives as our Forefathers did.
>
> (Robinson and Quinney, p. 10)

While the nation-to-nation process used between 'Indian' nations and European nations was upheld in the Royal Proclamation of 1763, which was to last 'as long as the sun shines, the grass grows and the water flows', the reality had been very different. Guarantees and provisions of sovereignty for First Nations Peoples have been almost totally ignored and conveniently overlooked by the Canadian Government and its Department of Indian Affairs. Reserves were reduced in size, even occasionally arbitrarily (and illegally) entirely relocated. By the 1960s there was even discussion of the 'extinguishment' of Treaty Rights and Treaty status.

'Termination' in the USA, 'extinguishment' in Canada, it seemed that total assimilation was inevitable and the loss of the distinctive languages, culture, beliefs and cosmologies of First Nations Peoples only a matter of time!

BROKEN SPIRIT

The traditional political structure of the First Nations was replaced at a stroke, when in Canada the Indian Affairs officers and in the USA the Bureau of Indian Affairs were given absolute jurisdiction over all decisions pertaining to development, education and the way of life of the people. In Canada, Aboriginal Peoples were not regarded as citizens but as wards of the state, and not even accorded federal voting rights. Yet their own First Nations political structures were systematically rendered powerless and ignored, despite localized resistance. Compare the following figure with the one shown in 'The Sacred Circle of Life' chapter (page 28), and notice how each social function was taken over and run by the dominant society.

The Broken Hoop. Under the impact of colonization all the prestigious social roles were taken over or replaced by the dominant society

The social (family and clan) structure was weakened and destroyed as children were forcibly removed from their parents and placed in residential schools, frequently never to return. Other children were sent by Child Welfare agencies for adoption into non-Aboriginal families. Between 1971 and 1981 a total of 3,729 Canadian 'Indian' children were adopted by non-Indian families. For thousands of these young people, culture and language were lost for ever. Many of the younger generation, raised in white society, grew up knowing nothing of their own culture and were taught to view it as primitive and shameful.

To try and understand what it felt like to grow up on a reserve, in a society where the people were totally disempowered, and saw no options for viable economic activity other than the demoralizing welfare cheque, or moving out into the predominant mainstream society only to encounter racial prejudice, here are some excerpts from a letter written by Laverne Jacobs.

A LETTER FROM LAVERNE JACOBS

I grew up some forty years ago on the Walpole Island Reserve, the southernmost reserve in Canada. The Walpole Island Band is an amalgamation of several Indian tribes or First Nations – the main ones being Ojibway and the Pottawatomie. During my early years I lived in idyllic ignorance, basically unaware of life outside the reserve. My world consisted of my parents, grandmother, brothers, sisters, aunts, uncles and many cousins. As children my brother and I hauled water from an outside well. During the fall and winter we helped our mother or father saw logs and chop them into firewood. Homework was done by the light of an oil lamp.

However, one does not remain a child for ever. One loses one's innocence all too soon and reality hits home. When I was eight years old my father, in search of employment, moved the family to the nearby city. It was there that I first heard the term 'Redskin'. It was there that I began to know that I was different.

The teen years brought even more pain. As my world enlarged and grew beyond the boundaries of family, I became acutely aware of the many social problems which beset my community. The most overwhelming was the problem of alcohol. On weekends my parents would take us into the nearby town of Wallaceburg to do the weekly shopping. As we waited to catch the bus home I would see many of my people staggering down the streets, others holding up the street lamps and still others engaging in fights and loud behaviour. I would see and feel

*Geese, which mate for life, are rejoicing. The four feathers represent the
four directions and the sweetgrass, among its many good things, represents a unity –
a binding together of many strands*

the scorn on the faces of the white people. I felt so utterly ashamed. How I wished I could change the colour of my skin.

The effects of these social conditions upon the youth were clearly evident in my brother's art. One year the Recreation Committee sponsored a contest to design a crest for Walpole Island. My younger brother drew a crest in the shape of a shield. In the centre of the shield was a bottle. Trapped inside the bottle was an

Indian. Arched over the bottle was a banner with the inscription 'Walpole Island Recreation'!

The alcoholism only aggravated the racial tension that existed between the reserve and the local town. The racism was heightened by the Canadian Government's assimilation policy and the move to integration during the 1960s. During this period my peers and I were bused to schools in the nearby town. For most students this proved to be a rather traumatic experience. Cultural differences such as an oral tradition and the non-competitive nature of Indian people gave rise to them being labelled 'dumb Indians'. Teachers were often quite insensitive and racist.

For many people during this period, tragedy and hardship was a way of life. There would be deaths by shootings or alcohol-related accidents. Poor health conditions resulted in time spent in tuberculosis sanatoriums. A strange and often unjust judicial system gave rise to repeated incarcerations for minor infractions. Poverty sometimes meant a diet of porridge and 'Indian Bread' with a spread of lard and salt. For many the only way out of such conditions was the bottle.

At that early age little did I realize that this social malaise was only a symptom of a much deeper problem: the loss of one's land, culture, dignity and spirituality.

These God-ordained gifts fell victims to European domination, colonialism and paternalism. Every aspect of Indian life was under federal control and the despised 'Indian Act'. This Act, a product of the Canadian Federal Government, determined who/what was an Indian. It defined the systems of local government or Band Council. It bestowed upon one man, a white 'Indian Agent', enormous powers. He was the Justice of the Peace, the Truant Officer and the Band Administrator with authority to veto any resolution of the Band Council.

The power and control of the Indian Agent is one I will always remember. My parents once looked forward to building a new home. Dad sent away for some house plans. Together he and my mother chose the plan of their liking. The foundation was poured . . . when along came the Indian Agent who requested to see the plans. He said that they were too elaborate and would have to be changed.

By the late twentieth century, 500 years of suppression have resulted in a legacy of seemingly intractable problems. Of the First Nations populations living on reserve lands in total (USA and Canada) over one-third of all residents live below the poverty line. Unemployment is endemic, reaching over 90 per cent in the more isolated and resource poor areas. Alcoholism, domestic violence and child abuse rates may be over 80 per cent on some reserves, illness rates are soaring, and accident, murder and suicide rates are two or three times the national averages.

> Many books have been written on the plight of Indian people. So many that the spirit and vitality of our people is often suffocated by them. We have been probed, prodded and analysed as if an autopsy were being performed on dead people. Few people are willing to look behind the devastating statistics of our poverty, unemployment, high suicide, alcoholism, cancer and mortality rates, poor housing, inadequate education, high proportion of prison inmates, etc. etc. etc. Few people see the life which has kept us going despite these deplorable effects of colonialism.
>
> (Robinson and Quinney, p. 2)

6 | MENDING THE HOOP

> Healing for Indigenous people means a number of significant things. Their minds must be healed from the ravages of centuries of oppression. Their bodies must be reclaimed from alcohol and abuse, both sexual and physical. Their spirits must be reclaimed, the spirit of their ancestors, not the spirit of Christianity or any other doctrine. It means all of these things and all of these things at once. From our experience it is possible to do this. We have found where psychoanalysis, conventional therapy, and other means of dealing with people's problems have failed, there is one way that has consistently given results and that has changed people's lives profoundly, giving them a renewed sense of self, a stronger foundation to face the world and a vision for the future. This way entails the reclamation of their understanding of themselves as Indigenous people and their role on this planet.
> (Clarkson, Morrissette and Regallet, p. 47)

During the early and mid-1960s, Native people in both the USA and Canada began to speak out for self-determination. They discovered that they received an increasing amount of public support as people became more aware of the injustice of their situation. The time was ripe. Revisionary works of North American history were recounting, not a history of glorious progress, of courageous pioneers and settlers of high moral worth establishing lands of freedom, opportunity and justice. Instead, histories of deep, unredeemed tragedy and failure were emerging in which the legacy of lands taken by violence, massacre, genocide, trickery and theft from Native peoples are but one example of a fundamental ruthlessness, greed and short-sightedness at the very heart of North American civilization. The legacy of slavery and the Vietnam War are other examples.

An important step in public awareness and support in the USA occurred at the conference convened by the Native peoples at the University of Chicago in 1961. Attended by over 500 natives from 70 USA tribes, plus Canadian and Mexican observers, it called for the end of paternalism, and for assistance in establishing their own programmes and policies in such fields as economic development, education and health. This conference also saw the establishment of the National Indian Youth Council (NIYC), devoted to promoting Indian political issues and culture, which rapidly grew to over 26,000 members.

In 1966 the Cherokees banded together to protest the abrogation of their treaty rights and many non-Indians shared the feelings expressed in the following declaration:

The Declaration of the Five County Cherokees of Oklahoma

Now we shall not rest until we have regained our rightful place. We shall tell our young people what we know. We shall send them to the corners of the Earth to learn more. They shall lead us. . . .

In these days, intruders, named without our consent, speak for the Cherokee people. When the Cherokee government is the Cherokee people, we shall rest.

In these days, we are informed of the decisions other people have made about our destiny. When we control our destiny, we shall rest.

In these days the High Court of the United States listens to people who have been wronged. When our wrongs have been judged in these courts, and the illegalities of the past have been corrected, we shall rest.

In these days, there are countless ways by which people make their grievances known to all Americans. When we have learned these new ways that bring strength and power, and we have used them, we shall rest.

In these days we are losing our homes and our children's homes. When our homeland is protected, for ourselves and for the generations to follow, we shall rest.

In the vision of our Creator, we declare ourselves ready to stand proudly among the nationalities of these United States of America.

Similarly, in Canada, a new feeling of hope and cultural regeneration began to emerge, phoenix-like, after decades of suppression and cultural genocide. Despite a depressing history, and no doubt encouraged by events in the USA, a new sense of hope and of determination was emerging among Canadian First Nations Peoples. Also a new generation of well-educated and vocal leadership began to challenge old assumptions, and question both the legality and the justice of government policies. This is evident in the following declaration:

A Declaration of the First Nations (Canada) November 1981

We the original peoples of this land know the Creator put us here.

The Creator gave us Laws that govern all our relationships to live in harmony with nature and mankind.

The Laws of the Creator defined our rights and responsibilities.

The Creator gave us our spiritual beliefs, our Languages, our culture, and a place on Mother Earth which provides us with all our needs.

We have maintained our freedom, our Languages, and our traditions from time immemorial.

We continue to exercise the rights and fulfil the responsibilities and obligations given to us by the Creator for the Land upon which we are placed.

The Creator has given us the right to govern ourselves and the right to self-determination.

The rights and responsibilities given to us by the Creator cannot be altered or taken away by any other Nation.

(Robinson and Quinney, p. xv)

In both countries, with the increase in cultural pride, and a growing public support for improved conditions on the reserves, Native school enrolment began to increase steadily. In the USA, college enrolment increased from a mere 2,000 in 1960 to over 30,000 in the mid-1980s. With more educated and professional members, including Native lawyers, doctors and education officers, communities were better able to formulate and articulate their grievances, document their land claims, and press these claims through the courts. However, a wide gap still exists between the relatively few well-educated leaders, elders and professional people, and the majority of those living on reserve lands.

Today over half of North America's First Nations Peoples live in urban areas, outside of the reservation lands recognized by the two federal governments. Among this modern, youthful and often activist group are many who are ready to take strong confrontational measures to bring their plight to the media and public attention. In 1969 one of the earliest dramatic confrontations was when young Native activists, calling themselves 'Indians of All Tribes', occupied the abandoned prison island of Alcatraz for over nineteen months, pointedly offering the USA government $24-worth of beads.

New activist groups formed quickly in both the USA and Canada. And in 1970 President Nixon called for 'Indian' tribes to assume full independence, and control of their own organization and lives, without being cut off from Federal support.

> Nixon's words ushered in one of the most active periods of Indian legislation in American history. The United States Congress passed a steady flow of new laws that mandated increased spending for Indian schools and health care, established a federal responsibility for the protection of religious practices, recognized long-moribund fishing rights, and conveyed large tracts of federal land to native corporations in Alaska.
>
> (Bordewich, p. 84)

Meanwhile militant groups continued to grow more vocal and dramatize their plight to a more receptive population. The American Indian Movement (AIM) documented the Trail of Broken Treaties, which was taken to Washington by a militant group that broke into and vandalized the US Federal Bureau of Indian Affairs before the 1972 elections.

In 1973 about 200 youthful, armed militants disputed with tribal elders at the village of Wounded Knee, South Dakota, where in 1890 between 150 and 300 Sioux had been massacred by the US cavalry. Surrounded by FBI agents, federal marshals and droves of media cameras they held out for 71 days, eventually leaving two Indian militants dead and one marshal wounded.

In 1975 the pivotal Indian Self-Determination Act was passed in the USA. Over 150 petitions were immediately received from groups seeking offical tribal status. In 1977 The American Indian Review Commission carried the concept of sovereignty a step further, stating:

> the relationship of the American Indian tribes to the United States is founded on principles of international law. . . . That Indian tribes are sovereign political bodies, having the power to determine their own membership and power to enact laws and enforce them within the boundaries of their reservations.
>
> *(Ibid.)*

In the census of 1990, nearly two million Americans listed themselves as 'Indians'. Over one million of them are members of federally recognized tribes. Each recognized tribe enjoys a direct government-to-government relationship with the USA. It also receives assistance in establishing a formal tribal government, tribal courts, police and schools. And freed of federal and state regulations, yet still faced with urgent economic necessities, tribes can and do turn their lands into anything from casino and resort developments to nuclear waste dumps! By the late 1990s more than 160 USA tribes and several reserves in Canada (such as Rama, Ontario) were operating casinos. The most profitable to date is that of the 320 member Mashantucket-Pequot Tribe in the hills of Connecticut. They now own one of the largest casinos in the world, employing a staff of more than 9,000 and grossing about $800 million annually.

In the USA the basic question posed by the current situation was well summarized in the Final Report of the American Indian Policy Review Commission of 1977.

> Today we must ask the central question: Is the American nation – now two hundred years old, and one hundred full years beyond the era of the Little Bighorn – yet mature enough and secure enough to tolerate, even to encourage, within the larger culture, societies of Indian people who wish to maintain their own unique tribal governments, cultures and religions?

It would seem the answer in the USA has been generally a 'Yes'. Over 300 self-governing tribes (that number is still increasing) are directing their own affairs with greater or lesser degrees of success. The Cherokee nation is an example of a very successful development.

AN EXAMPLE OF REVIVAL: THE CHEROKEE NATION

The Cherokee Nation, once a pastoral people, quickly accepted many ideas from the white settlers around them. At the start of the nineteenth century they occupied over 60 villages in the south-eastern US, scattered from Alabama through Georgia to Tennessee. In 1817 their administrative capital was built at New Echota (now in north-west Georgia, which in 1817 was outside the frontier of the USA). It had an elected legislature, free press and thriving trade. In 1826, the city recorded some 762 looms, 2,488 spinning wheels, 172 wagons and 2,943 ploughs. In 1827 they established an elected model of government, and adopted their own constitution. The USA had signed treaties with the Cherokee, guaranteeing their territorial integrity.

However, in 1802, to persuade Georgia to reliquish claims to land areas in other states, and as a prelude to large-scale white land settlement, Thomas Jefferson agreed to the systematic removal of all Indians from the state. In 1828 gold was discovered in the heart of Cherokee County, and Georgia State annexed the Cherokee land; two years later they declared Cherokee laws to be null and void, and Congress passed the removal bill.

Then the Cherokees, in an unprecedented move, sued the State of Georgia. In 1832 the US Supreme Court found the Cherokee Nation to be 'a distinct community, occupying its own territory, with boundaries accurately described, in which the laws of Georgia can have no force'. It upheld the Cherokee Nation's right to exist. However, this was totally ignored by Georgia, which parcelled out their land to whites, and herded them into stockades, where over 2,000 died before the march west began. In 1838 they started out for Oklahoma along what has become known as the Trail of Tears, with another 4,000 people dying en route.

Once in Oklahoma they rebuilt the nation in the foothills of the Ozarks, with a new centre of Tahlequah. Here they organized a prosperous community well ahead of the standard way of life of the surrounding European settlers, and by 1840 were enjoying a golden era of progress. The Cherokee Nation was formally terminated in 1906.

The Cherokees were among the first USA tribes to accept the Bush administration's offer of 'self-governance' – to manage their own affairs independently of the Bureau of Indian Affairs.

Today the Cherokee Tribe is a success story. The people are proud of their Native status and cultural heritage, while being 'intertwined inextricably with the culture, economy and people' surrounding them. With an annual operating budget of over $75 million, derived mainly from the tribe's own enterprises such as hotels, retailing outlets, and manufacturing (including component parts for IBM,

General Dynamics, and the US Army, among others). Tahlequah, its political and administrative centre, is a city of about 17,000, which every year since 1985 has won a certificate for excellence of financial reporting.

(Based on accounts in Bordewich)

In Canada the situation is somewhat different, although there is the same ever-growing determination by more and more First Nations Peoples to press their land claims through the judicial system and courts, and to dramatize their plight to win public support. A very dramatic event was the 1990 'Oka Crisis', involving the defence of the Tall Pines on Kanehsatake tribal land, on the outskirts of Montréal (Quebec), which was being taken to make a golf course. The media across Canada and round the world were treated to stunning pictures of over 2,000 Quebec Provincial Police and Federal troops laying siege to a tiny community where a small band of defenders, mainly unarmed women and small children, stood guard over their ancestral land.

In Canada, First Nations rights have frequently emerged as key issues within the complexities of the Constitutional debate. Each of the original tribal treaties was made between two sovereign nations – that of the particular tribal council concerned, with that of the British crown. In all attempts to repatriate and reformulate the constitution, Aboriginal Treaties and rights have been ignored. Today the First Nations of Canada are reasserting their independence and sovereignty, and the validity of the original treaties agreed between two sovereign powers. It remains to be seen if they will, as in the USA, achieve political autonomy – a new, third sphere of sovereignty (in addition to the Federal and Provincial powers).

The 1996 Report of The Royal Commission on Aboriginal Peoples to the Government of Canada strongly advocated a radical and fundamental change in the relationship between the Canadian Government and First Nations Peoples, and moving rapidly towards their self-government.

> Commissioners believe that the door to Aboriginal group participation in Canada has been opened by recognition of an inherent right of self-government in the common law of Aboriginal rights and in the treaties.
> (Vol. 1, p. xxvi)

However, the sovereignty and political independence (currently enjoyed by USA Registered Tribes) comes at a price. Tribal politics and financial accounting may be deemed closed to external scrutiny. There is no longer any guarantee of basic human rights for individuals, or democratic participation, or of the separation of legislative, executive (police), and judicial functions. Tribal councils, while receiving large payments of public money, need not be accountable, nor open their books to auditing. In the case of injustice, misappropriation of funds, or discrimination, there is no external court of appeal where redress might be sought.

In 1997, aware of these problems, Canadian federal officials began conducting a review of financial practices on all Canadian reserves. First Nations are directly responsible for the management of 83 per cent of the $3.3 billion of public funds transferred to them annually, to cover welfare, housing and all other programmes. Clearly there must be accountability, and a built-in method of auditing.

Inevitably, other serious philosophic issues arise whenever 'self-government' or 'sovereignty' of groups within a larger nation are discussed. What does it mean to be politically independent, while still dependent on financial assistance, goodwill and defence capability of the larger nation? What is the status of non-Natives living on reserves? Other issues are concerned with the morality of extending or restricting benefits and services to certain groups on the basis of race, and what does 'Native Race' mean? After 500 years of contact, intermarriage and migration, it is doubtful if any 'pure' Indigenous or Aboriginal people still exist. What then is the basis of claiming 'Native' status – lineage, marriage, adoption, residence?

The dramatic occupations and military confrontations not only awoke the general public to the issues, they also gave First Nations Peoples an increased pride in their traditions and heritage. A vast number of local Native organizations have been formed; tribal groups established their own land claims offices; urban groups organized Friendship Centres and in some cases organized their own security patrols. Today, increasing numbers of people, both Native and non-Native, attend and participate in pow-wows, traditional ceremonies, and healing circles. Increasing numbers are speaking and teaching their traditional languages.

The rebirth of traditional cultures and the resurgence of Native spirituality has given many a new pride in their heritage. It has also empowered many bands to initiate court actions for long outstanding land claims, and to re-establish and further develop traditional forms of art, from totem-pole carving to weaving, from pottery making to lodge and longhouse construction.

Throughout the 1990s a revolution and resurgence of epic proportions has been under way throughout First Nations societies across North America. One First Nations group after another is aggressively pressing land claims through the courts, rediscovering their histories and cultures, and exploring different avenues towards economic and political independence. It is clear that in both countries Native Peoples are destined to play not only increasingly important, but also self-determined political and economic roles.

'Indian country', at the end of the 1990s, is no longer a series of neat little areas marked on a map, totalling about 4 per cent of the land area of North America. But as Bordewich claims, it is *less a physical landscape than it is a confusing snarl of jurisdictions and conflicting powers that nearly defies human ability to unravel.*

However, considering the enormous challenges that face First Nations Peoples in trying to free themselves from control in every aspect of their lives, it is essential to understand how the revival of their spiritual traditions has played a basic and fundamental role in this struggle.

A prayer

Finally, Sonkwaiatison (our Creator), we ask that you give us all the courage, the strength and the wisdom to use the power of the good mind in all that we do.
. . . and so it is, Sonkwaiatison, that we have reflected on our place within the Circle of Life and on our responsibilities to all of Creation. Life continues, and we are grateful for what we have.
So be it on our minds.

(Prayer from one of the 'Thanksgiving Addresses' which formed the opening and closing ceremonies of approximately 100 meetings of the Canadian Royal Commission Hearings on Aboriginal Peoples)

TASHUNCA-UITCO 'CRAZY HORSE' (1849?–77)

Sketch of model of Crazy Horse carving, Black Hills

Tashunca-Uitco was an able warrior, tactician, and a chief of the Oglala Sioux, who steadfastly resisted the tide of settlers steadily occupying the Northern Plains of the USA. Crazy Horse, as a small boy, was present at the massacre of a settlement near Fort Laramie, Wyoming, on 19 August 1854. In retaliation for this raid the American forces destroyed Sioux villages like Ash Hollow the following year, massacring women and children.

The Sioux were first offered the Black Hills in exchange for the rest of North and South Dakota, Wyoming and Montana! But even as they were being herded into this small area, gold was discovered in 1872 in the Black Hills. Sioux villages were burned, and the people, continually harried by American troops, either starved or were wiped out by European diseases or in battles.

Crazy Horse joined Sitting Bull and others and gathered a band of followers around him that developed into the Sioux Confederation. When the bands, starving and under attack from soldiers and settlers, refused to settle on the reserve lands, General George Cook surprised the Indian camp in mid-winter and drove off their ponies. Crazy Horse recovered the herd and moved north to defeat General Cook on the Rosebud river in 17 June 1876, and went on to annihilate

Colonel George Custer and the Seventh Cavalry on the Little Big Horn on 25 June 1876. Not one white man of the Colonel's 250 soldiers survived.

While Sitting Bull and other Sioux left their tribal lands for Canada, Crazy Horse remained in Sioux territory, pursued by Col. Nelson S. Miles. In May of the following year he surrendered and was promised limited freedom, but was stabbed in the back and fatally wounded by one of the prison guards.

South-west of Rapid City, in the Black Hills National Forest (26 km from Mt Rushmore), the visitor may stop at a viewing verandah, along Highway 385, and, surrounded by billboards, fast food emporiums and souvenir stands, can view a vast 'Work-in-progress' – the carving of an entire mountain into an unbelievably huge statue of the famous 'Crazy Horse'. The family of the late sculptor Korczak Ziolkowski continues work on the memorial begun in 1909. When completed, the mountain carving will stand 563 feet high, and 641 feet long.

Bullhead mask of Born-to-Be-Head-of-the-World

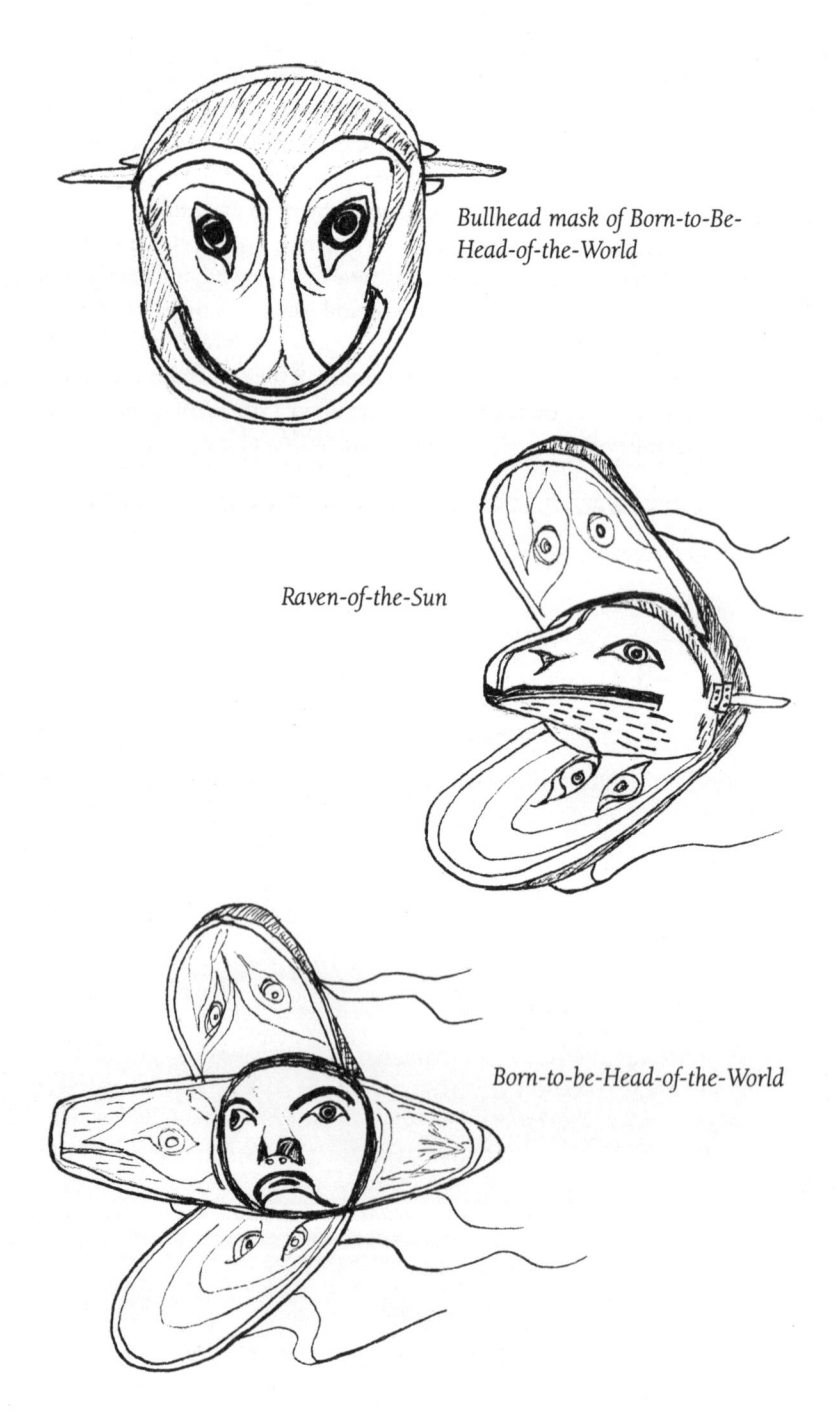

Raven-of-the-Sun

Born-to-be-Head-of-the-World

Kwakiutl mask that opens

66

7 | HEALING THE SPIRIT

The resurgence of traditional Native spirituality is essential to the restoration of self-respect, cultural pride, and the rebuilding of community. It is needed for the ongoing fight to reclaim land, and restore treaty rights. It is needed also to maintain the ongoing demands for repatriation: of the children taken away for adoption, of art and artefacts seized for museum and art collections around the world and, in some cases, of the bodies of ancestors plundered by archaeologists, and the return and restoration of grave sites and sacred places.

Among some Native societies, and especially the Ute, Apache, Navajo and Pueblo Nations of south-western USA, many of the traditional teachings and rituals, from creation myths to healing chants, sand painting rituals to dances with kachina masks, remain virtually intact and unchanged. Even though many Pueblo people attend Roman Catholic services, they see nothing contradictory in practising the two religions simultaneously.

At the other extreme are numerous communities where ancient traditions are irrevocably lost, particularly those of the south-eastern USA where those not totally eliminated by European diseases and warfare were displaced from their lands in 1830, and forced westwards along the 'Trail of Tears'.

Others, like the Canadian west coast communities, have reinstated ceremonies, dances, and traditions such as the potlatch that were formerly banned. In so doing they reinvigorated the ancient arts of carving, heraldry, dancing and costume manufacture.

In the east,

> Many Iroquois in New York State and Canada still follow their old beliefs as codified and reformed in 1799 by the Seneca prophet Ganyodaiyo ('Handsome Lake'). This religion is influenced to some degree by Quaker beliefs, but it is essentially Indian. Ceremonies are conducted in Iroquois longhouses and are closely tied to farming and the seasons; only Iroquois languages are used, although virtually all Iroquois people are now English-speaking.
>
> (R.D., p. 396)

In many communities almost all the people are now adherents of some denomination of the Christian church. Even Black Elk in his later years was a Catholic catechist. The Native American church, which is the most widespread religion among US Native Peoples today, is also found in Canada. The church tenets combine traditional Native and fundamentalist Christian elements. The cross, the trinitarian nature of God and baptism, are all based on Christian beliefs, while the most important sacrament is the eating of the buttons of the peyote, a hallucinogenic cactus, in order to induce contact with the supernatural. The peyote, which grows wild in Mexico and the American south-west, can produce visions that often take the form of beautiful, kaleidoscopic design and is most influential among the Plains tribes, for whom the vision quest has long been an important ritual. Yet while sacramental use of other drugs, such as alcoholic wine in many churches, and the smoking of marijuana among Rastafarians, has been legalized in the US, in 1988 and 1990 the US Supreme Court held that the First Amendment, protecting freedom of religion, did not protect Aboriginal sacred sites and burial grounds, nor permit the religious use of peyote by the American Native Church.

Some degree of syncretism is inevitable over half a millennium. And, as might be expected, some mainline churches incorporate important aspects of Native tradition and history into their practices and liturgies. The Kateri Tekakwitha Society, named after a Native Canadian saint, is an important movement within the Catholic Church, while the head of the United Church of Canada from 1992 to 1994, the Very Revd Stan McKay, is also a highly respected Native elder.

To many youths, however, the quest to discover and restore their own Native spirituality is the quest to discover their roots and identity. It is a search for spiritual wholeness in the midst of soaring addiction and suicide rates and social disintegration. It is often a quest fraught with pain, confusion and division – the legacy of paternalistic and colonial churches wrongfully engaged in the suppression and destruction of another culture. There is thus the anomaly of many young people being more open to the ancient traditions than are their elders who were raised in the Christian church.

A marked trend over the last couple of decades, and surely a hopeful sign of a growing mutual respect, is the new interest of mainstream North American communities in the traditional faiths of the First Nations Peoples.

> While one could hardly expect wholesale conversions to native ways, still it seems evident that the Native American view of nature and of spirituality are affecting white society in ways that would previously have been unthinkable. Some of this influence is rather superficial, of course, particularly that associated with the 'new age' true believers. But there is evidence that many Europeans and European Americans are willing, indeed eager, to learn more about tribal spirituality.
>
> (Versluis, p. 8)

Despite the variety of cultures and traditions, it is possible to generalize, for some aspects of traditional belief transcend tribal differences.

Nature is sacred

Nature is experienced as hierophanic, that is, manifesting a spiritual presence. And certain aspects of nature, e.g. a particular bird, animal, star or mountain, will be regarded as sacred because of their ability to transmit revelation to a particular person or clan. While each tribe and clan has its own sacred sites and creatures, all recognize that the material, visible world is an embodiment of the spiritual, invisible realm.

Thus, nature should be treated with reverence and respect, for it is a manifestation of spiritual power – Orenda (Iroquois), Manitou (Algonquin), Wakan-Tanka (Sioux), Kachina (Hopi). Respect and thankfulness for the gifts that nature provides are the proper human attitude.

Rituals and ceremonies permit people to participate in the annual cycle of seasons, and in the cycle of human life. For the Pueblo peoples it is in the complex annual cycles of masked dances, ceremonies and accompanying mythologies that participants learn their true place and purpose on this Earth.

> These cycles and masked dances represent the union – the indivisibility – of the human, the animal, the spirit and the celestial worlds. They form a liturgical cycle that in fact reveals spiritual presence in the natural and human world.
> (Versluis, p. 21)

Shamanism

Shamans or 'Medicine Men' are men or women who act as intermediaries between the spiritual and material worlds to effect healing. While practices and manifestations of shamanism vary greatly, it is central to almost every First Nations traditional belief system throughout the Americas. Some shamans may well be trained in Western medicine or nursing but, in addition to these skills, will draw on a profound knowledge of local herbs. They are concerned not only with physical healing, for which many patients go first to a clinic or hospital, but also with holistic healing of body, mind and spirit. The healing extends to the well-being of communities as a whole, and to helping people to rediscover their role in the hoop of the community, and the larger hoop of creation.

Their expertise goes way beyond Western physical and psychiatric therapies, as they apply ancient wisdom and spiritual tools to help in healing victims of disease, abuse, addiction and despair. Through solitude, communing with nature, fasting, prayer, purification and self-discipline, shamans undertake journeys into the spiritual realm, receive visions, dreams, messages and the power of healing to bring back. Many experience a spiritual death and resurrection. All have a special relationship to animals, especially to their particular totemic species (e.g. owl, bear, or eagle) who will appear to them, guard them and give them wisdom.

For all shamans the pattern is similar. They go alone into nature (perhaps to a hill), go into a trance, 'travel' to the spirit world, seek help and assistance for the one who is ill, come back and announce their vision and effect the healing. Many work with extraordinary success, are highly respected in the community, and may join chaplaincy teams in hospitals and prisons.

For an example of shamanism, look at the story of Sedna (pages

81–2). When sea animals and fish become scarce, the Inuit shaman (or angakuk) is called to journey to the bottom of the sea, down an axis towards the centre of existence, to where Sedna, the keeper of the sea animals, dwells. Combing her hair will please her and she will release the animals and fish again.

Instead of going on a spiritual journey, the Algonquin shaman (or jossakid) calls the animal spirits towards himself. The spirit presences become apparent in a mysterious and powerful manifestation known as the 'shaking tent'.

Among the Iroquois are found Midêwin secret lodges. During their lifetime, initiates ascend through hierarchic levels (usually four), each one more difficult and costly. Entry into each is through a ceremony symbolizing death and rebirth. At the highest level (whose totemic animal is the sacred bear), all members are considered shamans, and are shown great respect and sought after for healing.

While attitudes to nature and to shamanism are almost universal among First Nations in the Americas, ceremonies and rituals vary widely. Here are three examples of widely different ceremonies.

1. KACHINAS AND CEREMONIES OF THE AMERICAN SOUTH-WEST NATIONS

The American south-west is a land of spectacular deserts, towering rock pinnacles, mesas and canyons, with scorching heat and bone-chilling cold. Here the Pueblo nations – Hopi, Navajo, Zuni and Apache – follow a comparatively traditional way of life. The cycle of the agricultural year is spent in raising crops of corn, squash, tobacco and beans, and performing the ceremonies that ensure the health and prosperity of all living things, people and crops alike. Basketry, fashioning and decorating pottery, silver jewellery, and weaving rugs have been developed to a fine art. Tourism may now be added to this list, and much exquisite artistic work is destined for the tourist market.

The Hopi ('Peaceful Ones') have maintained a continuously occupied settlement at Black Mesa for over a thousand years. So passionate is the commitment to their traditions and communities that in 1680 they organized the only completely successful rebellion against the invaders. Under Popé, a medicine man from the Rio Grande Pueblos, the villages became united and staged a successful uprising against the missionaries and Spanish administrators, until 400 lay dead and scores of mission churches and settler homes were reduced to ashes. Then they lay siege to Santa Fé, routing the Spanish who retreated to El Paso. Again in 1700 they attacked a village where missionaries had settled, killing over 700 people.

Traditionally the villages or pueblos were built into the sides of high and defensible sandstone cliffs. The houses or hogans are women's domain, they own them, as they do the seeds and crops. The children, male and female, belong to the mother's clan, and on marriage the husband will move into his wife's home.

The most important buildings in the village are the kivas, and these are the men's domain. They are stone-walled ceremonial chambers, partially below ground, or in ancient time sunk deep into the ground beneath the village plaza. Although the Spanish tried desperately to destroy them because of their spiritual importance, many of the ancient holy chambers still exist, some at abandoned sites, but many others in active use. The kivas symbolize the Worlds Below, from which the Spirits first emerged to fill the Earth with all things animate and inanimate, and it is to the World Below that people return after death. It is from the kiva that the kachinas emerge.

The term 'kachina' has come to refer broadly to any masked figure. It generally also refers to the spirit beings who mediate between the humans and the spirit worlds, the masked dancers who personify them, and even to the carved and decorated wooden kachina dolls which are given to the children.

In the kivas the men create, learn and rehearse the kachina songs and dances. Ordinary masks are made by their owners and are often re-decorated for each performance. The Mond (Chief) kachina masks, however, are permanent and considered to be ancestral figures containing great power. The masks are kept in the kiva for half the year until Soyal (the winter solstice) when they are brought out and worn for ceremonial dances until Niman, five days after the summer solstice, after which they are returned to the World Below.

Niman is a sixteen-day festival led by members of the Hemis kachina cult. The mask of Hemis (Far Away) carries the symbols for rain and bountiful harvest. Kachinas are used in the February celebration of Powamu, which turns the attention of the community to the upcoming agricultural season. They are also used at night dances in the kiva during the winter season, and at plaza dances as soon as it gets warm enough. Plaza dances have become very popular with tourists. Each of the thirteen Hopi villages maintains more or less similar ceremonial cycles.

Later in the year the Snake Dance and Flute Dance are performed by men. Central to Hopi life is the belief that all things in nature have specific roles to play in maintaining the world's equilibrium. People's task is to keep good hearts and observe the complex rituals to ensure that all goes well. Of the numerous rituals, the Snake Ceremonial is one of the most spectacular, when for four days men go out collecting snakes of all kinds from the desert. Then a myth and dance ritual is enacted with the snakes being held in the dancers' mouths for four circuits of the plaza. Finally the snakes are taken back unharmed and released. The purpose of the ritual is to assure an abundant harvest.

Other rituals such as the Marau ceremony are performed by the women's societies. Marau is a nine-day ceremonial that includes the preparation of special pahos boards painted with designs of clouds, corn and Muyinwa, who personifies germination and growth.

The cycle of human life, like that of the agricultural year, requires ceremony at birth and naming, during childhood, at adolescence, puberty, marriage and death. Both the girls' Kinaalda and the boys' Wuwutcim ceremonies are designed to mark the passage to adulthood and to instruct in the duties and responsibilities of adult life.

Another whole group of ceremonies are associated with healing. Sand painting is frequently performed during the final days of eight- or nine-day healing rites. A clean sand base is prepared in the centre of the ceremonial hogan. On this base coloured, crushed minerals are placed to construct intricate designs and patterns of the mythological figures relevant to the particular ceremonial being used. The completed painting is blessed by sprinkling pollen or cornmeal on it from the four cardinal directions. Then the One-sung-over, for whom the ceremonial is being performed, walks into the painting and sits in the middle of it. The singer (hataalii), conducting the ceremony, applies the sands from the painting systematically to their feet, legs, body and head, in the process destroying the painting. Meanwhile the hataalii is singing the associated songs of great heroes, of creation, and of the ways of the world.

The Blessingway (Navajo) is a one-night song and prayer

ceremony performed for good fortune and a long and healthy life. It is often performed at birth and wedding celebrations, at a girl's Kinaalda, house blessing or travel blessing. Almost all of the other mythological and ceremonial complexes are used for healing. They include: the Chiricahua Wind Way, Hailway, Enemyway (one of the few ceremonials performed during the summer, directed towards any Navajo whose illness is attributed to contact with the enemy). Night Way, one of the most complex and elaborate myth and ritual healing complexes, includes public outdoor dancing during two nights. Where Night Way ends, the Mountainway myth and ritual healing complex begins.

Most of these ceremonials and beliefs and practices were relatively unknown to the general public beyond the borders of the southwestern reserves until they were popularized by the series of mystery novels by Tony Hillerman. These novels awakened a growing general interest and sympathy for an alternative and clearly durable and environmentally respectful and sustainable view of the world.

2. THE POTLATCH OF THE WEST COAST NATIONS

Kwakiutl, Nootka, Haida, Tsimshian, Tlingit, Salish and other nations of the Pacific north-west live in an environment that abounded in coastal fish, marine mammals and water-birds. Abundant fish from the great salmon runs, whether consumed fresh or dried, provided a dietary staple. The forests not only provide wildlife but supply materials for house construction and the production of great figurative carvings: totem and mortuary poles, house decoration, carved boxes, canoes and the dance masks for which these nations have become famous. The people exploited the waters and their riches with such success that it took only part of the year to provide themselves with an annual food supply and with a surplus for trading. There was thus time available for weaving blankets, carving, and organizing the feasts and ceremonies in which wealth and social rank could be lavishly displayed.

The most important of the ceremonies was the potlatch, an institution that stood at the very centre of their culture, and was unique in having no exact counterpart in any other known culture.

The potlatch was a feast of several days' duration, with guests numbering into the hundreds. Feasting was followed by elaborate dances, in which the host had dancers dressed in fabulously carved masks, depicting ancestral legends and stories that validated the chief's claim to title and rank. This was followed by a lavish 'give-away', the distribution of gifts to all the guests. Gifts would include furs, food, jewellery, carved boxes and bowls, that might have taken many years to accumulate. Acceptance of a gift formed an unwritten contract that the recipient had witnessed and validated the potlatch of their host. While validating status and major family events of the host, the potlatch also provided a valuable means of wealth redistribution. It was assumed that the recipient would pay back the gift twofold at a later date.

Following contact with European settlers in the late nineteenth century, and the decimation of the population by European diseases, the remaining people began to move to settlements clustered around the Hudson's Bay Co. trading posts and to participate in the wage economy. While some traded furs and fish, others were employed in canning plants, and much of the money earned this way was spent on increasingly large and competitive potlatches. The most valuable gifts were antique 'coppers', or carved copper plates, signifying one's rank, history and family relations. A single copper might be valued at over 9,000 Hudson's Bay blankets. Very rarely a chief might destroy his property or break a copper as a sign of authority and wealth. The broken pieces might be offered to family members and to a rival chief, who then had to break one of greater value or be humiliated.

The potlatches grew ever larger with thousands of carvings, bracelets, and sacks of flour, mountains of canned biscuits, furniture, household appliances and blankets being given away. A misunderstanding of white settlers about the nature of the potlatch, and also the fact that giving and generosity were qualities in conflict with their individualistic and consumer-based values, led to the Canadian Government passing legislation to ban the potlatch in 1884. Two years later, in a speech at Fort Rupert, Franz Boas stated 'It is a strict law that bids us dance. It is a strict law that bids us give away our property. It is a good law.' A time of fear and confusion followed the ban. During the dark days of potlatch prohibition, the people persisted in carrying on their ceremonies in secret, although altered in ways that secrecy demanded. In 1922 twenty people were imprisoned for two months for potlatching. Two of those imprisoned lived to see the end of the government prohibition of potlatch in 1951.

Following the 1884 ban, museums and wealthy white collectors managed to acquire many hundreds of priceless dance masks, and other carvings, including almost all the coppers. Since 1951, there have been requests for the return of these artefacts from some of the world's leading museums of anthropology. Some have been returned, while some others have been loaned back and can be seen in the U'mista Cultural Centre at Alert Bay and the Kwagiulth Museum near Campbell River. Today the potlatch is once more going strong. The first 'legal' potlatch was held by the Salish in 1953. As one of the survivors of the 1922 trials said:

> When one's heart is glad, he gives away gifts. It was given to us by our Creator, to be our way of doing things, we who are Indians. The potlatch was given to us to be our way of expressing joy. Every people on earth was given something. This was given to us.

In Alert Bay, various tribes contributed towards the design and construction of their own 'big house'. It was completed in 1963 and was opened with a potlatch hosted by Chief James Knox of Fort Rupert, one of those imprisoned in 1922. Since then there have been potlatches every year, not only in Alert Bay but also in big houses in Kingcome Inlet, Gilford Island and Comox. For villages that have not yet built big houses, potlatches can be held in community halls, but people comment that it is just not the same without the earth floor and the central fire.

The reasons for holding potlatches today are much the same as before – naming children, mourning the dead, transferring rights and privileges, and occasionally celebrating weddings or the raising of memorial totem poles. The big house in Alert Bay holds about 700 people; guests usually come for the weekend, and none leave empty-handed. Although people generally have jobs, and children are in school, so that potlatches cannot last for a week, they usually begin in the afternoon, so that mourning songs may be sung before sunset, and will continue throughout the following day and into the night. Today, master carvers continue to make spectacular masks for the traditional dances and the young people can learn of their ancestral heritage, and see the ancient stories and legends enacted in spectacular presentations in the flickering firelight of the big houses, and participate in the feasting and give-aways.

3. TEACHINGS OF BLACK ELK IN THE PRAIRIES AND EASTERN WOODLANDS

If the communities of the American south-west have maintained their traditions and ceremonies in an unbroken culture for over a thousand years, a very different situation occurred across the great expanses of the prairies and vast taiga forests that span the continental interior where nations such as the Cree, Ojibwa, Lakota and Algonquin saw their traditional way of life almost totally eliminated. On the open plains of the prairies their economic base was shattered when the buffalo were destroyed, and their land bases diminished as reserve land was taken for farming. In the forested regions, land was clear-cut by forestry corporations, exploited by mining and tourist operations, and thousands of square miles of the most productive wildlife areas were flooded beneath hydroelectric dams. Their cultures were eroded, languages lost, and religious ceremonies made illegal and suppressed.

Only since the 1970s has there been a revival of the old sacred traditions and values. The search for historic authenticity blends with the need to reconstitute a coherent belief and associated ritual system that has meaning for today's youth who are now facing the devastating social conditions, engendered by poverty and despair.

Black Elk's Vision has become one of North America's greatest religious classics. Black Elk described all of the more important ceremonies that are most widely practised on the Plains. In the account of his famous youthful vision Black Elk recounted how he was carried to a rainbow-covered lodge, the Lodge of the Six Grandfathers (this symbolized the powers of the four cardinal directions, plus the sky above and the Earth beneath). Each of the six grandfathers blessed him and gave him symbolic gifts: life-giving rain, the cleansing power of snow and sacred herbs, the sacred peace pipe, a tree seedling for the centre of the nation, the yellow hoop of all things and last of all the spirit of Mother Earth.

Black Elk saw in a vision that the Earth was becoming sick. The four-legged and winged ones grew frightened, and all living things became gaunt and poor. The air and the water became polluted. And in the midst of the destruction he was shown a blue man who was causing the damage and Black Elk was called to overthrow him. He was also shown his own people over a great span of time. In ancestral times he saw them as 'a good nation, walking in a sacred manner, in a good land'. Later they became disunited and followed different paths – he and his people had become captives of the dark reservation road, and he saw miserable, starving faces and people sick and dying. At the end of Black Elk's great vision he was promised that his people would once more be free and would help to spread the power of peace and understanding. Then Black Elk said:

> And I saw that the sacred hoop of my people was one of many hoops that made one circle, wide as the daylight and starlight, and in the centre grew one mighty flowering tree to shelter all the children of one mother and one father. And I saw that it was holy.
>
> (*Black Elk Speaks*, p. 43)

He also told how White Buffalo Calf Woman came to the Sioux, and gave them seven sacred ceremonies, most of which are still practised. Then she held out to the people her sacred bundle in which was the pipe, the most important gift of all.

The pipe is the most treasured possession of spiritual elders, both women and men. They train and work for long to acquire wisdom and knowledge and earn the right to be a pipe carrier. Each pipe (many of which are decorated with eagle feathers) is held in great reverence, and is kept in its own pipe bag to be brought out and used by its owner at all sacred ceremonies. 'The pipe is us', said one Sioux. 'The stem is our backbone, the bowl is our head. The stone is our blood. When we partake of the Sacred Pipe, we are sharing our breath – and our souls – with the Great Spirit.' This is the most widely practised ceremony both on and off the reservations. It is used to open meetings, and at sweat lodges, Sun Dances and naming ceremonies.

Tobacco, the first of the sacred herbs, is offered to the Great Spirit, to Mother Earth, and to our grandfathers, grandmothers and ancestors, to the living and to the yet-to-be-born. It is sprinkled in the four directions seeking blessing before the pipe is smoked. It should always be presented out of respect as a gift to spiritual elders when approaching them with a request. The other sacred herbs include cedar, sage and sweetgrass.

The Sweat Lodge Ceremony has become the one most frequently practised. Its primary purpose is purification from sins and from brokenness, thereby restoring the harmony between people and the elements of earth, air, water and fire. It is held both on and off the reserves, with increasing numbers of non-Indian people participating. The lodge itself is easily constructed from saplings bent together to form a half sphere about the size of a small room, and four to five feet high. The entrance always faces east, the direction of the rising sun. Traditionally covered with hides or buffalo robes, the saplings are now usually covered with a thick layer of blankets and tarpaulins that completely exclude the light. The floor may be sprinkled with sage or cedar twigs, and a shallow fire-pit is dug in the centre. A drum and other instruments such as turtle shell rattles and eagle bone whistles may be used. A few feet in front of the entrance, to the east, a sacred fire will be burning, in which a number of large rocks are heated.

The participants (usually eight to sixteen people) will come wearing very light, simple clothing, and after offering tobacco will enter the lodge to sit in a circle around the fire pit. The red-hot rocks are brought in, the flaps are closed down and the ceremony begins. After drumming and offering songs and prayers to the six directions, and to the three times (to the ancestors, the living and the yet unborn), each person in turn can speak of what is troubling them and then pour cold water upon the red-hot rocks. Clouds of fragrant steam soon fill the lodge. After several rounds, or 'endurances', the flaps may be opened and fresh air, more hot rocks or more cold water brought in, and the ritual repeated.

While the sweat lodge itself is simple to describe, it is almost impossible to convey the profound spiritual, healing and psychic experiences of the participants. Here is how one elder describes the experience:

> The spiritual bond is likened to an attachment to Mother Earth as one sits in her warm womb. It can be a key function in the search for a spiritual link to God's creation – nature, the environment.
>
> The four directions are called upon within the lodge. The misty, fire-heated steam covers you, bringing forth your own mist (your sweat). The waters of the world, which have been brought into the lodge, join and mix with the air of the four directions. . . . The four winds will carry the life blood out of the lodge to the four quarters of our planet. . . . I personally equate the Inipi (Sweat Lodge), as the ceremony that intermingles and conveys the lifeblood of the world. Water is the lifeblood of this ecosystem of fire, water, air, and earth – the four elements.
>
> (McGaa, p. 62)

The Sun Dance, long banned, saw a rapid and spectacular recovery in the 1980s. Traditionally it is the annual coming together of the community to give thanks to the Great Spirit. In the days of preparation, the construction of the dance arena and the shady arbour of poles and pine branches surrounding it, making special dance clothes, the collection of sage for the dancers' wrists and ankles, the building of sweat lodges, the community is strengthened in unity, common purpose and thanksgiving. During the entire four days of the dance, participants fast. It is a time of endurance and bravery that builds a sense of accomplishment and pride both in the dancers and in their families.

The Sun Dance Chief is always a highly respected spiritual teacher. First a sapling is cut and set up in the centre of the arena, symbolizing the axial centre of existence, linking the Earth and the spirit world. Beneath it, or on the axial pole, several buffalo skulls will be placed. The pole itself is decorated with coloured ribbons representing the four cardinal directions, the sky above and the Earth beneath.

At dawn each morning the dancers enter the sweat lodges, then purified, put on their simple and comfortable dance clothes. Dancers may be of any age from quite small children to octogenarians, and most will dance to the steady rhythms of the drummers throughout the entire four days. Often non-Native people will be permitted to participate in the ceremony. On the fourth day some of the young men (spiritual warriors), as a test of courage and bravery, may request piercing. Only those who are approved and deemed ready may come forward, one at a time, to have a wooden peg inserted through the loose flesh of their back. Ropes are attached to the peg and then tied to a series of buffalo skulls. The dancer will then attempt to run forward dragging the skulls behind him as fast and as far as possible before the peg tears out. The one who drags the most skulls the furthest distance receives great honour and is awarded a trophy.

The Give-Away. Traditionally, following his death, a warrior would be buried with his most prized possessions. A current version is for the closest relative to hold a Give-Away Dinner for friends and relatives on the first anniversary of the deceased's departure to the spirit world. In addition to distributing the possessions of the deceased among the guests, the feast-giver may have spent a large part of the year in making and purchasing additional gifts for all of the invited.

Healing Circles and Healing Lodges are becoming very important in the healing and recovery of victims of physical and sexual abuse, those trapped in alcohol or drug addiction, and those released from reform school or prison. Here they can be introduced to the sacred ceremonies, participate in sweat lodges, and rediscover their place in the community. Often, when all are seated in a circle, a 'talking stick' or eagle feather is passed slowly around the circle. Everyone in turn can speak for as long as they are holding the 'talking stick' and are listened to by the rest. Slowly trust is built up within the circle which permits the expression of pain and hurt, of grief and anger.

A prayer

Perhaps it may be, and this is my prayer, that through our sacred pipe peace may come to those people who can understand, an understanding which must be the heart and not the head alone. Then they will realize that we Indians know the one true God, and that we pray to Him continually.

We should understand well that all things are the works of the Great Spirit. We should know that He is within all things: the trees, the grasses, the rivers, the mountains, and all the four-legged animals, and the winged peoples; and even more important we should understand deeply in our hearts, then we will fear, and love, and know the Great Spirit, and live as He intends.

(Black Elk – Oglala Sioux)

SEDNA – THE WOMAN WHO LIVES UNDER THE SEA
An Inuit myth from the Canadian Arctic

Sedna is one of the most important figures in Inuit mythology. As a young woman she married a hunter who revealed himself to be a powerful shaman. He took her far away and provided for her only a poor shelter of fish skins. She spent the winter in misery, cold and hungry.

In the spring her father came to visit his daughter, and when he saw her unhappiness he rescued her. On the return journey, however, the shaman followed their boat, creating a violent storm. Terrified, her father threw Sedna overboard. Desperately she swam in the freezing Arctic water and after a supreme effort she reached up and clung to the side of the kayak to pull herself in. But her

First Nations Faith and Ecology

father, seeing this, snatched up his axe and chopped off her fingers and then her hands. Sedna sank back to the bottom of the sea, where she transformed herself into the most powerful of the spirits. Her severed fingers became seals, whales, walrus, fish and bears, all the living creatures of the land and sea.

From the bottom of the sea Sedna determines the worthiness of the people before she permits the animals to give up their spirits to the hunters. When her people are bad towards one another Sedna withholds her creatures and the people hunger and starve. It is said that all the sins of the people get tangled in Sedna's hair. Because she has no hands, a shaman must go down to the bottom of the sea and comb her hair clean. This makes Sedna happy and she once more releases her animals, and the people have good hunting. Both bounty and misfortune come from the Keeper of the Sea.

In 1990, the Royal Trust Co. commissioned four carvers (George Pratt, Simata Pitsiulak, Philip Pitsiulak and Taqialuq Nuna) to carve a huge statue to Sedna for their corporate headquarters office building.

That summer the four carvers and their families encamped on Baffin Island and, using power tools, crowbars and picks, cut a series of huge slabs of pink and grey marble from a rock seam beside the Arctic Sea. There they began carving the larger-than-life figures of Sedna, the shaman, bear, seal and walrus. The carvings were moved by sea around the coast and down the St Lawrence River to Montreal, where they were finished and placed in the building lobby.

Healing the spirit

NAVAJO SAND PAINTING

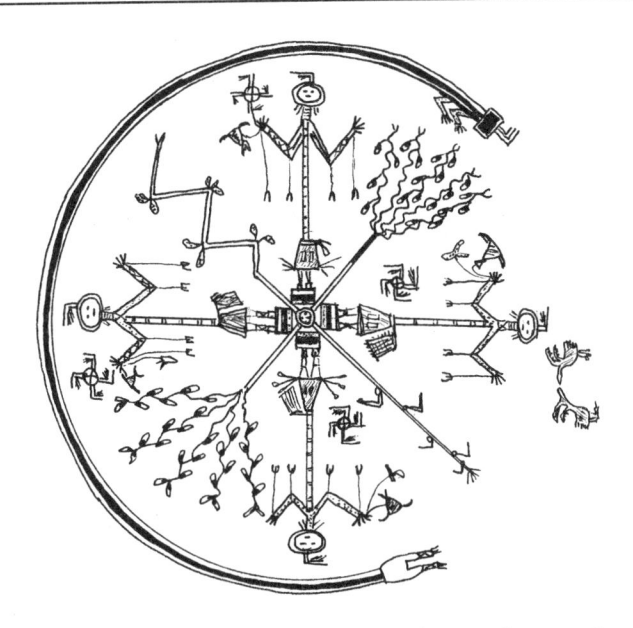

Navajo sand painting from the Yeibachi or Night Way Chant

Among Pueblo Peoples such as the Navajo, Hopi and Zuni elaborate sand paintings are prepared as part of a healing ceremony that also includes chanting, dancing and serving a meal to participants. When all is ready, and the sand painting is prepared, sacred pollen and corn meal may be sprinkled and the one who is sick will be led out to sit in the centre of the painting, as lengthy healing chants are sung.

Navajo – 'A Prayer of the Night Chant'

House made of dawn.
House made of evening light.
House made of dark cloud.
House made of male rain.
House made of dark mist.
House made of female rain.
House made of pollen.
House made of grasshoppers.

First Nations Faith and Ecology

Dark cloud is at the door.
The trail out of it is dark cloud.
The zigzag lightning stands high upon it.
An offering I make.
Restore my feet for me.
Restore my legs for me.
Restore my body for me.
Restore my mind for me.
Restore my voice for me.
This very day take out your spell for me.

Happily I recover.
Happily my interior becomes cool.
Happily I go forth.
My interior feeling cool, may I walk.
No longer sore, may I walk.
Impervious to pain, may I walk.
With lively feelings, may I walk.
As it used to be long ago, may I walk.

Happily may I walk.
Happily, with abundant dark clouds, may I walk.
Happily, with abundant showers, may I walk.
Happily, with abundant plants, may I walk.
Happily, on a trail of pollen, may I walk.
Happily may I walk.
Being as it used to be long ago, may I walk.

May it be beautiful before me.
May it be beautiful behind me.
May it be beautiful below me.
May it be beautiful above me.
May it be beautiful all around me.
In beauty it is finished.
In beauty it is finished.

(Navajo Chant from *Native American Traditions*, edited by Sam Gill)

Scarred ailing Mother Earth. Native woman offers prayer and the sacred herbs: tobacco, sweetgrass, cedar and sage. The eagle feathers and eagles are sent to 'defend the land'

8 THE LAND: RAVAGE, REPATRIATION AND RESURRECTION

Hayden Burgess (Hawaiian) has stated:

> The Earth is the foundation of Indigenous Peoples, it is the seat of spirituality, the fountain from which our cultures and languages flourish. The Earth is our historian, the keeper of events and the bones of our forefathers. Earth provided us with food, medicine, shelter and clothing. It is the source of our independence, it is our Mother. We do not dominate her; we must harmonize with her.
> (Quoted in La Duke)

In both political and economic discussions First Nations Peoples have invariably considered the welfare of the community as a whole, and of future generations, rather than the rights of the individual or corporation to make a short-term quick profit.

Finding themselves holding to radically different understandings of Earth and of human–spiritual–land relationships from the dominant North American majority, First Nations Peoples have been a persistent and amazingly consistent force. They have not ceased to confront government, business, and church agencies with an alternative world-view, despite unceasing reductions to reserve lands, and attempts to extinguish treaty rights.

Growing out of this long history of oppressive colonization, during which their lands were either taken, sold or 'developed' by others, First

Nations Peoples have grown to perceive themselves as guardians of Mother Earth. Thus they have found themselves in increasingly frequent situations of conflict with corporations, and government agencies seeking to 'develop' the 'resources' by destructive means such as clear cutting the forests, damming the rivers, strip mining, and weapon testing. Only a few examples can be selected as illustration.

Weapon testing

In 1863 the Treaty of Ruby Valley, later confirmed in 1869, designated an area of 43,000 square miles as Newe Sogobia, property of the Western Shoshone Nation. Yet since 1963, the US has conducted some 670 weapon test explosions there. *And to maintain control over the area, the United States has usurped almost 90 per cent of Shoshone land.*

NATO training flights

In Labrador and north-west Quebec, about 10,000 Innu live in the area that they call Nitassinan. In the 1950s, they were forcibly resettled into villages, and compelled to give up their traditional hunting-gathering way of life, when the Churchill River Dam flooded ancient burial grounds and important areas of hunting territory. In the early 1980s the military base at Goose Bay, near the Innu village of Sheshatshit, was selected for NATO pilots to train in low-level flying. This involves planes flying as low as 30 metres from the ground. By 1992 there were almost 8,000 flights during the period April to November. Despite massive local resistance, in May 1995 the Canadian Government approved an increase in the number of annual military training sorties from 7,000 to 18,000, including 15,000 low-level sorties, and an expanded flying area of 130,000 square kilometres with additional bombing ranges. In addition, mining companies have recently filed 13,000 new claims covering thousands of square kilometres of land at Voisey Bay, despite Innu eviction notices to two companies.

Uranium mining and processing

In 1975, 100 per cent of all federally produced uranium came from Indian reservations, where there were no fewer than 380 uranium mining leases. With promises of jobs and 'development', the Navajo

Tribal Council approved a mineral agreement giving Kerr McGee Corporation access to uranium deposits in the Shiprock area. Wages for the 100 Navajo men employed in the mine were as low as $1.60 per hour, while an inspection of the workings reported radiation levels 90 times above the tolerable level. By 1980, 38 miners had died and many more had respiratory ailments and cancers. Cases of leukaemia and birth defects had escalated on the reserve.

> By 1980, forty-two operating uranium mines, ten uranium mills, five coal-fired power plants and four coal strip mines (spanning 20–40,000 acres each) were in the vicinity of the Navajo Reservation. Approximately fifteen new uranium mining operations were under construction on the reservation itself. Although eighty-five per cent of Navajo households had no electricity, each year the Navajo nation exported enough energy resources to fuel the needs of the state of New Mexico for thirty-two years.
>
> (Winona La Duke)

Fifty miles to the east of the Navajo Reserve is Lagun Pueblo, until 1982 the site of the world's largest uranium strip mine – the Anaconda Jackpine – which had covered 7,000 acres of the reservation by the time the most profitable uranium ores had been exhausted. The agricultural and ranching valley that provides food for the Pueblo is watered by the Rio Paguate river which runs through the abandoned mine tailings, emerging on the other side a fluorescent green in colour.

Coal strip mining

The North Cheyenne reservation is located in the centre of the largest deposit of coal in the USA. Although the Cheyenne have vigorously opposed strip mining for over 30 years, 'multinational energy corporations working with the approval of the federal and state governments are surrounding the Cheyenne reservation with coal strip mines, railroads, electric generating plants and transmission lines' (Winona La Duke). The reserve lands are adjacent to the Powder River Coal lease, the largest federal coal sale in the history of the US. It stretches from the Wyoming border, and runs along the major water source – the Tongue river.

At least five coal-fired power plants are on, or adjacent to, the Navajo-Hopi Reserves. The vast strip mine at Black Mesa ships coal to the Four Corners Power Plant – the only man-made object seen by Gemini Two astronauts from outer space. It causes falling levels and contamination of ground-water, but perhaps its most significant impact is the forced relocation of over 10,000 Navajo people from the area over the Black Mesa coalfield. There is no word for relocation in Navajo: 'to move away' simply means 'to disappear'.

Clear-cut logging

Across North America, from the western Queen Charlotte Islands to Quebec and the Maritimes, Native Peoples have been among the first to organize resistance to the destruction of forests together with their wildlife, streams and rivers, and the traditional way of life that depended upon them. From Temagami, Ontario, to Clayaquot Sound, British Columbia, struggle after struggle has seen increasing numbers of the general community joining Native people in passive resistance – blocking logging roads and bridges, using the press, public opinion and the courts to raise awareness of the vast scale and irreparable nature of the damage caused by these short-sighted policies.

For example, the Alberta Government granted the Japanese company, Daishowa Marubeni International, a twenty-year lease to 25,000 square kilometres adjacent to the Peace river, and another 15,000 square kilometres plus money for roads, railroads and a bridge. The company also purchased the rights to log the Wood Buffalo National Park, the last great stand of old-growth spruce in Alberta. These leases overlap with the traditional lands of the Lubicon Lake First Nation, who have been protesting to little avail.

Hydroelectric development

Today, almost all the major rivers in Canada and the USA have been dammed, despite growing public concern and Native resistance, from the vast dam on the Churchill river in Labrador, to the huge WAC Bennet Dam on the Peace river, British Columbia.

Mic Dam, Williston Lake, Lake Diefenbaker, Old Man Dam, Limestone, Jenpeg, Baskatong – names abound that conjure up some of the largest engineering works of the twentieth century and some of the greatest public protests. All, however, are dwarfed by the scale of the James Bay project in northern Quebec, introduced in 1972 at a projected cost of a staggering 10 billion dollars. The James Bay water basin contains rich ecosystems teaming with wildlife, provides the nesting grounds for migratory birds, and the feeding area for the largest migratory herd of mammals on the continent – the George's river caribou. Over 35,000 Native Peoples – Cree, Ojibway, Inuit and Innu – live in the area and depend upon its resource base for hunting, trapping, fishing and gathering wild rice and other products, as well as providing tourist services.

> The first stage of the project – James Bay I – concentrated along the Eastmain and Rupert Rivers ruined the ecology of some 176,000 square kilometres. The Native people of the area did not hear of the project until planning was well under way. Following years of futile litigation, 400 kilometres of paved road, three power stations, and five reservoirs were built. Four major rivers were destroyed and five 735 KV powerlines cut a swath through the wilderness...
>
> (Winona La Duke)

If Phase 2 continues, it will impact a further 356,000 square miles, and an entire ecosystem will have been destroyed.

The unending struggle for the environment

The Gwichin Nation, on the Alaska–Yukon border, together with a coalition of environmental groups, managed to avert the opening up of the Arctic National Wildlife Refuge to oil exploration in 1991. The 19 million acre refuge, referred to as America's Serengeti, is essential to the Porcupine caribou herd (170,000 animals). Oil which could be exploited in the Gwichin territory represents probably fewer than 200 days of US oil needs, yet if exploited would devastate the calving grounds and Arctic ecology of the Wildlife Refuge. Legislation to open the reserve to oil drilling was narrowly defeated in the US Congress in 1991, and as world oil reserves are consumed, it will fall under increasing pressure.

Indigenous peoples have so far been on the front lines of the North American struggle to protect the environment against the destruction and pollution that follow from colonialism, militarism, and industrialization. As many treaties are being upheld by the courts, and significant land areas returned to First Nations Peoples, the question still remains open as to how they will respond to twenty-first-century demands, both of their own people for development, and of the world for resources.

> Tribes are being forced to come to terms with the practical nature of their relationship to the land, to decide as a matter of policy whether the earth is primarily a form of wealth to be converted to goods, services, community welfare, and personal income, or whether it is something wholly different.
>
> (Bordewich, p. 136)

In the USA at least 50 per cent of all uranium, between 5 and 10 per cent of all the oil and gas reserves, and one-third of all the strippable low-sulphur coal deposits lie on reserve land. Since the USA Self-Determination Act of 1975 the Navajos of Arizona and the Jicarilla Apaches of New Mexico have established their own tribal oil and gas commissions to regulate production on their lands. The Southern Ute Tribe of Colorado has set up its own oil production firm. Colville Confederated Tribe of Washington trained staff to manage tribal timberland on a sustained yield basis. The Confederated Tribe of Warm Springs, Oregon, now owns three hydroelectric dams and sells power to the state grid. But there are other, more encouraging examples.

THE PAIUTES

The Paiutes had lived for over 1,000 years around the oasis of Pyramid Lake in the Northern Nevada Desert, a lake where trout and the cui-ui (a snub-nosed relic of the Pleistocene) abounded.

As new cities and irrigated agricultural projects like Newlands sprang up in Northern Nevada, Derby Dam was constructed to meet the growing demand for urban and irrigation water. The results were catastrophic! Deprived of water, Lake Winnemucca grew smaller and eventually disappeared, marshes dried up, wildlife disappeared, and Pyramid Lake dropped about 80 feet and its spawning runs began to fail. By mid-century it seemed clear that the extinction of the cui-ui was inevitable. The Paiutes saw its fate as indistinguishable from their own. 'The cui-ui was their flag, their nation, their identity', claimed the fish hatchery manager Paul Wagner.

The Paiutes wanted more of the water to raise the lake level for the cui-ui to survive. California State demanded more water for further development around Lake Tahoe, Nevada State claimed more water, and the nearby towns of Reno and Sparks required increased water supplies for urban expansion. But unexpectedly, the cui-ui became one of the first species to be placed under protection by the 1966 Endangered Species Act.

Following years of litigation, in 1990 the USA Senate approved a settlement.

It awarded $43 million to the small Fallon Tribe of Paiutes, partially to improve their irrigation. Both water and water-rights were removed from the Newlands irrigation project, rendering the project no longer viable. This increased the level of Pyramid Lake and ensured the survival of the cui-ui. In addition to a $25 million fund created to operate the tribal fisheries, another $40 million was set aside for economic development on the Pyramid Lake Reservation. This settlement also gave the Paiutes rights as equal partners in the water management of the entire Truckee Basin. It has been commented 'The settlement was a philosophical water-shed, supporting "a new ethic of place", which tries to balance stable, improved economies with respect for the environment and the rights of Indian tribes. An ethic of place (that) respects equally the people of the region, the land, animals, vegetation, water and air . . . and includes a dogged determination to treat the environment and its people as equals, and to recognize both as sacred.'

ANCESTORS, ARTEFACTS AND LAND CLAIMS

Ancestors

In 1989, the Bush administration redefined the responsibility of the Smithsonian Institution, America's most prominent museum – and by implication all other museums of archaeology and the entire nation – towards its Native population. It was ordered to make a complete inventory of all human remains and funerary artefacts, numbering in the hundreds of thousands, and to make them available for 'repatriation' to the Native peoples to whom they originally belonged. All objects found in excavations on tribal or federal land 'automatically became the property of whatever Indian group could reasonably lay claim to them', and trafficking in human remains and cultural items was declared a federal crime. As ancestral bones and artefacts were repatriated 'home' to be reinterred, proximity to the spirits of the ancestors gave tribal people encouragement and a feeling of cultural continuity and revival.

Artefacts

Artefacts 'collected' during colonial times by soldiers and collectors were regarded as trophies, loot, prizes of power. Anthropologists and scientists justified their collections, assuming that North American Native Peoples would soon disappear from the Earth. But not only were Native peoples increasing numerically, they were gaining political and economic power, and cultural values were also changing. Such artefacts were being seen as illegal fruits of imperialism, their acquisition unethical, if not downright criminal.

All artefacts were ordered to be immediately returned to the descendants of the original owners, or to their tribes, if no relatives could be found. Many Native people saw this as the 'liberation' of still living and powerful things that had been imprisoned in museum basements 'in limbo between the spirit world and the human'. Some even attributed centuries of suffering to the captivity of the spirits. In 1990 the Hopi reported that up to two-thirds of their sacred artefacts had been stolen. In New York a stolen dance mask or war god might easily sell for $100,000.

In 1989 New York State handed back twelve wampum belts to the Onondagas, who claimed them as being of sacred value. The Peabody Museum returned to Nebraska 'Waxthe'xe', the sacred pole of the Omahas, the white buffalo robe and about 150 other artefacts. When the sacred pole (a simple cottonwood pole), the central symbol of Omaha identity, was displayed for the first time in a century on the pow-wow grounds at Macy, hundreds lined up to touch it, many weeping openly. A few turned away, afraid to lay eyes on something so powerful.

THE RETURN OF AHAYUDA

Once a year, at the winter solstice, members of the Zuni Bear and Deer clans carve new pairs of Ahayuda, also known as the 'Terrible Two' or the 'Boy Gods of War'. They are slender, humanoid figures about 18 inches high, who are living embodiments of the twins who led the emergence of the Zunis from the underworlds. Placed in clumps around the settlements, and looking remarkably like weathered fence posts, they acted as lightning rods, catching and warding off evil forces.

In 1968 the Zunis began systematically contacting museums, private collectors, auction houses and even the FBI, requesting the return of Ahayuda to the Pueblo. Claiming that the war gods' captivity had dire consequences, not only for the Zunis themselves, but for all humanity, they went on to explain: 'We Zunis are not a dead culture that stopped evolving in the 1880s. . . . Putting a war god under glass is not preserving culture. The way you preserve Zuni culture is by using the war gods in the living ritual for which they were created.' Furthermore, all Ahayuda belong to the tribe and no individual has ever had the right to give away or sell them. Therefore, by definition all Ahayuda not on tribal land were stolen.

In 1978, federal agents halted the auctioning of a Zuni war god in a New York gallery, and since then several dozen more Ahayuda have been returned from prestigious museums throughout the USA. For the first time, museums are being challenged to make a distinction between art and objects of religious veneration.

Land claims

There is hardly a First Nations group in either the USA or Canada that is not establishing its own land office, and researching centuries-old treaties, ancient records of their histories and sacred places, to establish a legal claim to tribal recognition and registration, treaty rights and land claims.

Literally hundreds of land claims are currently filed and awaiting hearings in Provincial, State or Federal courts in both Canada and the USA. Many are vast in scale, and historically and legally complex. Many take years to sort out before a judgement can be made and then, if it is an unfavourable one, it will be appealed. In total the area within British Columbia currently being disputed includes virtually the entire province. One of the largest claims now before the courts is the joint Wer'swetsen and Gitxsan Peoples' claim to an area of 57,000 square kilometres in the central interior of the province (that is, an area approximately the size of the entire province of Nova Scotia).

In USA the Lakota Sioux are claiming the entire area of the Black Hills as their exclusive property, based largely upon the 1868 Fort Laramie Treaty. Although their claims were dismissed with apparent finality in 1942, in 1979 the court reversed its decision, and offered payment for the land at 1876 prices, plus damages, together with accrued interest on this amount, which totalled some $106 million. Although the money was promptly rejected, the courts banked it in the tribal name, so that it has now grown to over $350 million, sitting untouched and rejected. The Lakota Sioux have now strengthened their case by claiming that the Black Hills are a sacred place, profaned by white exploitation. Although they were very recent arrivals in the area at the time of the Little Big Horn battle, many claim the hills to be 'the foundation of Indian religion', and that Wind Cave marks the site of Sioux emergence into the world. Thus they demand, not money or compensation, but the return of the hills in their entirety. In 1996 Bordewich (p. 234) commented that 'the Sioux campaign to regain the Black Hills has already succeeded in quite an unexpected way, transforming them from a shaming reminder of all that had been lost into a modern symbol of collective salvation'. Although the hills may not have been sacred in the past, they are now! The antiquity of a belief is not important, what matters is the relationship between the people and the shrine.

As an example of the complexities and unforeseen ramifications that may arise unexpectedly, it is difficult to find a better case than that associated with the attempt to build an observatory on Mount Graham.

MOUNT GRAHAM

In the USA, Mount Graham, Arizona, was chosen in the early 1980s as the ideal site for a major international observatory to be constructed by a consortium that included the University of Arizona, Germany's Max Planck Institute of Radioastronomy, the Arcetri Astrophysical Observatory of Florence, Italy, and the Vatican Observatory. In 1985 the University of Arizona wrote to eighteen Indian tribes in Arizona and New Mexico, inviting them to comment on the environmental impact statement. None replied except the Zunis, whose delegation to the mountain found only three long-abandoned shrines, which the University promptly segregated from the worksite. However, in 1990 the Apache tribal council unexpectedly stated its opposition to the project. Enlisting the support of environmentalists, and a group called the Apache Survival Coalition, they have succeeded in holding back the development for the better part of a decade, claiming that any disturbance of the mountain is a form of sacrilege.

A major protest campaign enlisted the support of the Audubon Society, and the National Council of Churches, among numerous other organizations. Suddenly people were prompted to compare Mount Graham to Sinai, Ararat and Olympus. The mountain was declared to be the sacred source of the Apache religion, although the Apache peoples only arrived in the area shortly before the Spanish. Suddenly constructing an observatory 'would torment the Earth', would endanger a rare species of squirrel, would anger the spirits and cause much havoc, destruction, environmental collapse and increased cancer. The project was denounced as a form of 'spiritual termination' and as 'an insult to all Native Americans'. Equipment was set on fire, and workers videotaped. The furore prompted questions in both the US Congress and the European Parliament. Funds were cut, sponsors withdrew. After years of delay the University of Arizona and its associates cut back the original plan for seventeen telescopes on 60 acres to seven telescopes squeezed into six and a half acres (see Bordewich, pp. 204–19).

Mount Graham had evidently touched a raw nerve, for reasons that go far beyond anything that could have been reasonably anticipated. Beneath the rhetoric lay several sources of fear and guilt. Firstly an awareness of the injustices perpetrated upon the Indigenous population; and secondly, a deep conviction that industrial development is responsible for irreparable damage to world ecology, and has also destroyed much of social, human and aesthetic value, leaving humanity with a vast spiritual emptiness. Indeed Mount Graham had become much more than a mountain, it had become a symbol of the integrity of the ecological web of life, of primal spirituality and of human innocence. And the observatory had become more than a simple project, it had become a symbol for all development, for industrial society itself, for exploitation and pollution, and for all dehumanizing and anti-spiritual forces.

*Illustration representing ancestors, culture and pride.
Four feathers represent the four directions.
Seven stars represent the seventh generation.
The eagles soar*

9 | FAITH AND VISION

It is undoubtedly true that much of the Indigenous religious ritual and culture has been eroded over the past half a millennium since the arrival of Europeans in the Americas. In fact some tribes have been obliterated, and their cultures, languages and cosmologies are lost for ever. Yet the strong and growing revival of Native beliefs, and the renaissance of First Nations cultures from coast to coast in both the USA and Canada, give a firm basis for hope in the future. Almost all Native traditions affirm the sacred nature of the Earth and of all living things within the web of life. They stress essential values of respect for the Earth and for creation, respect for ancestors, respect for elders and responsibility for the community. Native religion teaches care for the Earth, and asks people to consider carefully how any developments might impact the following seven generations.

These teachings of primordial and essential values, and of the human role in a sacred and hierophanic creation, have not only displayed an extraordinary resilience, but have something vitally important to say to the modern world about the value and mystery of life.

The differences between the modern, materialistic and scientific world-view that stresses development and profits, and that of the First Nations Peoples, gave rise to the conflict that is at the very heart of the tragic history of the Native American Peoples. Will it be possible in future to avoid violent political conflict as occurred in the military clashes at Wounded Knee (USA) in 1973, or at Kanesetake (Canada) in 1990? Is it possible for the two cultures to live in mutual respect, each tradition enhancing the other's spiritual vision and deepening their understanding of primordial spiritual truth?

When the first Europeans arrived and explored the St Lawrence river and the Great Lakes, they discovered to the south of the great water known in Mohawk as Onhatariyo (Handsome Lake) five different nations forming settled, agricultural communities. These five nations were, from east to west, the Mohawk, Oneida, Onondaga, Cayuga and Seneca. To ensure a peaceful co-existence and resolution of disputes the five nations had formed the remarkable Iroquois Confederacy or League. After the Tuscaroras were driven from North Carolina, around 1720, they were admitted as the sixth nation. Each of the six nations had its own language, its own name, and its own history, but collectively they called themselves Haudenosaunee, People of the Longhouse. At its height in the seventeenth and eighteenth centuries the Six Nations Confederacy controlled an area covering thousands of square miles and extending from Quebec to Kentucky, and from Pennsylvania to Illinois.

Just south of the present city of Syracuse,

> is a 7,000 acre Indian reservation – all that remains of the Onondagas' national territory. As the central nation of the Iroquois League, the Onondagas have always been its Firekeepers, the host of its assembly. In the middle of their reservation stands a new hall, perhaps one third the length of the ancient one on the hill but still a large building made of logs. Here sits the oldest living parliament in the Americas, and one of the oldest in the world.
>
> (Wright, p. 118)

The *Peacemakers Great Law*, which maintained governance, was an inspired blend of elective and hereditary rights, or checks and balances. A Confederacy Council of 50 sachems, or lords, was chosen by the clan mothers – the Iroquois being matrilineal. Each longhouse was the home of a senior woman with her female kin, their husbands and children, in all anywhere from 50 to 100 people. The accounts of the League's origin were retold orally for centuries, with the guidance of wampum belts, and then began to be written down and recorded by the Iroquois themselves. Early in the twentieth century the Seneca ethnologist A. C. Parker gathered and published the text. Here is an excerpt from Parker's rendering of the Iroquois Constitution: (see Wright, p. 120):

From Iroquois Constitution, or the Great Law

> The Smoke
> of the Confederate
> Council Fire shall ever ascend
> and pierce the sky so that other
> nations who may be allies may see . . .
> Whenever the Confederate Lords shall assemble
> for the purpose of holding a council, Onondaga Lords
> shall open it by expressing gratitude to their cousin Lords . . .
> and they shall make an address and offer thanks to the earth . . .
> to the streams of water, the pools, the springs and the lakes, to the
> maize, and the fruits, to the medicinal herbs and trees, to the
> forest trees for their usefulness, to the animals that serve
> as food and give their pelts for clothing, to the great
> wind and the lesser winds, to the Thunderers, to
> the Sun, the mighty warrior, to the moon,
> to the messengers of the Creator who
> reveal his wishes, and to the
> Great Creator . . . ruler
> of life and health . . .
>
> Five arrows shall be bound together very strongly and . . .
> this shall symbolize the union of the nations.

In his introduction Parker wrote: 'Here then we find the right of popular nomination, the right of recall and of woman suffrage, all flourishing in the old America . . . centuries before it became the clamour of the new America of the white invader' (Wright, p. 120). Looking at this document today, it is astonishing to realize the breadth and vision of this Constitution. In order for nations to dwell side by side in harmony and peace down to the present day, the law not only encompassed polity but was inclusive of the spiritual, human and environmental dimensions of life. It also expresses gratitude and thanksgiving for the gift of life and the abundance of creation. Listening and taking notes while an Onondaga spokesman criticized the bickering of several bordering USA states and recommended the Iroquois Confederacy as a model, was the 38-year-old Benjamin Franklin, later to become a co-author of the American Constitution. Even the eagle on the United States shield is 'the Iroquois eagle and the bundle of arrows in its grasp originally numbered not thirteen but five' (Wright, p. 116).

It was possible for six nations, with different languages and traditions, to formulate a lasting confederation bound by a constitution. Should it not also be possible for all the First Nations Peoples, despite their differences, to formulate a general and fairly inclusive statement?

By the early 1970s, First Nations Peoples from all parts of North America were travelling widely. Many had lived in urban areas or had studied in universities and had become familiar with a multitude of different Native communities and cultures. Many began to take part in the summer 'pow-wow circuit', travelling the length and breadth of the continent to participate in various dances, contests and ceremonies, or to meet well-known elders or healers. More and more First Nations communities established an annual 'Indian Days' celebration, when their community hosted visitors from across the country. Gradually a polymorphous process began, that may be termed 'pan-Indianism', which provided people with a common set of cultural traits, institutions and symbols. As one Micmac woman commented:

> Communications between tribes are spreading rapidly as people feel freer to move about, to visit and to get to know each other better. . . . You can go almost anywhere visit any tribe and you will hear words like Great Spirit, Mother Earth, Grandmother Moon, Indian Corn, Mocassin, Peace Pipe, Drumming, Chanting, Feathers, Braids, Indian Time, and lately injunuity and traditional. Instantly we understand and feel at home.
>
> (*Micmac News*, p. 37)

Because of the vast scale and rapid escalation of environmental deterioration, the 1990s have seen several major global conferences held on environmental issues. Here is an excerpt from the Onondaga Nation's Endorsement of the statement made by the Indigenous Delegation at the Global Forum on Environment and Development for Survival, Moscow, USSR, January 1990.

TRADITIONAL CIRCLE OF INDIANS, ELDERS AND YOUTH

The Traditional Circle of Indian Elders and Youth endorses the concepts of the Indigenous Delegation presented at the Moscow Forum: that we are all children of the Earth, the Earth is governed by the great laws of the universe, and that we human beings are responsible for the neglect and violation of these laws.

We have agreed that there is now a crisis of life upon this planet because we, the human beings, have upset the balance of life-giving forces of the natural world, and have interfered with the structures and cycles of air, land and water.

We have challenged the laws of the universe that govern the natural world. We delight in our new technologies which reap harvests without regard to the life cycles of the natural world.

We speak of our children, yet we savage the spawning beds of the salmon and herring, and kill the whale in his home. We advance through the forests of the Earth felling our rooted brothers indiscriminately, leaving no seeds for the future.

Indigenous people possess many different cultures and lifestyles but all recognize they are children of Mother Earth, and that we receive from her our life, our health, the air we breathe, the water we drink, our food and our energy. Earth suffers ill treatment because of lack of respect. All of us can understand the importance of the health of Mother Earth, and all have a potential to enjoy our lives in greater harmony with the forces which create life.

Brothers and sisters, we must return to the spiritual values that are the foundation of life. We must love and respect all living things. We must have compassion for the poor and the sick. We must have respect and understanding for women and all female life on this Earth which bears the sacred gift of life.

We must return to the prayers, ceremonies, meditations, rituals and celebrations of thanksgiving which link us with the spiritual powers which sustain us, and, by example, teach our children respect.

We must re-learn the great lessons of tolerance, generosity and love that will bring us peace and a future for the seventh generation to come. The path to human survival requires that we embrace a new age characterized by a global cultural pluralism which celebrates all the races, ethnicities and religions of humankind. Indigenous cultures can help provide inspiration for a future in which love is extended beyond the confines of human society to embrace the natural world.

We are accountable, and shall be held accountable if we fail. Our responsibility is to protect Mother Earth. Nature is a seamless web of life in which all forms of life are related to all others – the birds, the fish, the trees, the rocks – we are all connected to that web.

Indigenous people are nature's representatives to the modern human community; a community which is destroying Indigenous life.

We the Indigenous people of the Earth, have long experience of living on agreeable terms with the Earth. Is it possible that we can share our ancient knowledge with other people? Yes, surely. We shall go together in trust, in confidence, in belief, and we shall save our souls. This is the key to salvation.

We are people of the Earth. Earth is our place. Let us believe in it; let us take care of it as we take care of our children, our parents and grandparents. We are people of the Earth.

We must remember that we receive the benefits of Mother Earth from the Creator, and that we have a great responsibility to care for her and heal her. We have this duty and privilege to carry out in respect for our ancestors and for the coming generation.

Daw Nay Toh.

There is a great spiritual hunger and need for reassurance among many in the dominant Western culture. Many people experience little satisfaction or even the possiblity for creativeness in their daily lives, and see their own culture as not authentic. A feeling of alienation within urban Western society and a growing anxiety about environmental degradation leads some to look to Native American cultures, hoping to find there an 'authentic' or unchanging, primal spirituality.

Unfortunately no such simple and static culture exists or ever did. Acculturation and syncretism occur to some degree in all cultures and faiths, and are occurring even more rapidly now at the end of the twentieth century with ever-improving communication, such as the Internet and television. These can be used to portray ceremonies, rituals, beliefs and mythologies and to transmit them from one society and culture to another with lightning speed. However, this can be viewed as a major strength of First Nations spirituality, for the ceremonies and teachings being revived, created and taught now are a direct response to the needs and problems facing people, and the world as a whole today. Many people find the environmental sensitivity and the inclusiveness of the Circle speak directly to their own concerns and needs.

> Whether traditions have been passed on since time immemorial, retrieved, adopted or invented, we must remind ourselves that they may have very

important significance to the indigenous participants themselves. It behooves us, therefore, not to make light of such cultural practices. Instead, we must treat them with the respect they deserve.

(Prins, p. 393)

Undoubtedly one of the most significant and influential religious classics to emerge in North America is *Black Elk Speaks*. In 1930 John Neihardt, poet laureate of Nebraska, met with the Sioux holy man Black Elk in what he later claimed to be one of the most memorable experiences of his life. In lyrical prose he recorded the magnificent vision the old man remembered from his youth, and his lifelong reflections on the experience of people being driven from their homes and land, continually attacked and harassed by military troops, and eventually defeated at Wounded Knee. The power and significance of these teachings is in no way diminished by accepting that in his later life Black Elk was a Catholic catechist.

First Nations Peoples are often presented as models of right ecological attitude and as born conservationists. One reason for this is the widespread popularity of 'Chief Seattle's Speech'. In both Europe and North America it is widely used in environmental literature, it is quoted in numerous books and brochures, used on videos and films, and has been translated into over a dozen languages. For many it has become the embodiment of all environmental ideals.

There is no doubt that Chief Seeathl (or Seattle) of the Suquamish and Duwamish Peoples was present at the Port Elliott Treaty negotiations of 1855, when large areas of his people's land were signed away for white settlement. His speech of welcome in 1854 to the newly arriving Commissioner of Indian Affairs for Washington Territory, Governor Stevens, was probably made in his native language – Lushotseed. Notes on the speech were jotted down by Dr Henry Smith, who did not publish it until much later in the *Sun* newspaper in 1887, commenting that his own English was inadequate to render the beauty of the Chief's imagery and thought.

The speech has subsequently been rewritten at least twice, and the version we now have was recreated from Dr Smith's version by the film scriptwriter Ted Perry in 1970. It is thus not surprising that it contains several inconsistencies. It is most unlikely that Chief Seattle, from the forested west coastal region, ever saw a prairie buffalo, and no railway was built in his region before 1869. It is not as a historical document, but as a present-day statement that it has become widely used and quoted both by First Nations spiritual elders and by environmentalists. It is thus a fitting statement with which to close this book.

10 CHIEF SEATTLE'S SPEECH[1]

The Great Chief in Washington sends word that he wishes to buy our land.

The Great Chief also sends us words of friendship and goodwill. This is kind of him, since we know he has little need of our friendship in return.

But we will consider your offer. For we know that if we do not sell, the white man may come with guns and take our land.

How can you buy or sell the sky, the warmth of the land? This idea is strange to us.

If we do not own the freshness of the air and the sparkle of the water, how can you buy them?

Every part of this Earth is sacred to my people. Every shining pine needle, every sandy shore, every mist in the dark woods, every clearing, and humming insect is holy in the memory and experience of my people. The sap which courses through the trees carries the memories of the red man.

The perfumed flowers are our sisters. The deer, the horse, the great eagle, these are our brothers.

The rocky crests, the juices in the meadow, the body heat of the pony, and man – all belong to the same family.

So the Great White Chief in Washington sends word that he wishes to buy our land, he asks much of us.

The Great Chief sends word that he will reserve us a place so that we can live comfortably to ourselves. He will be our father and we will be his children.

So we will consider your offer to buy our land. But it will not be easy. For this land is sacred to us.

The shining water that moves in the streams and rivers is not just water, but the blood of our ancestors. If we sell you our land you must remember that it is sacred and you must teach your children that it is sacred and that each ghostly reflection in the clear water of the lakes tells of events and memories in the life of my people. The water's murmur is the voice of my father's father.

The rivers are our brothers, they quench our thirst. The rivers carry our canoes, and feed our children. If we sell you the land, you must remember, and teach your children, that the rivers are our brothers – and yours, and you must henceforth give the rivers the kindness you would give any brother.

The red man has always retreated before the advancing white man, as the mist of the mountains runs before the morning sun. But the ashes of our fathers are sacred. Their graves are holy ground, and so these hills, these trees, this portion of the earth is consecrated to us. We know that the white man does not understand our ways. One portion of the land is the same to him as the next, for he is a stranger who comes in the night and takes from the land whatever he needs. The Earth is not his brother, but his enemy, and when he has conquered it, he moves on. He leaves his fathers' graves behind, and he does not care. He kidnaps the Earth from his children, he does not care. His fathers' graves and his children's birthright are forgotten. He treats his mother, the Earth, and his brother, the sky, as things to be bought, plundered, sold like sheep or bright beads. His appetite will devour the Earth and leave behind only a desert.

I do not know. Our ways are different from your ways. The sight of your cities pains the eyes of the red man. But perhaps it is because the red man is a savage and does not understand.

There is no quiet place in the white man's cities. No place to hear the unfurling of the leaves in spring or the rustle of insects' wings. But perhaps it is because I am a savage and do not understand. The clatter only seems to insult the ears. And what is there to life if a man cannot hear the lonely cry of the whippoorwill or the arguments of the frogs around a pond at night? I am a red man and do not understand. The Indian prefers the soft sound of the wind darting over the face of a pond, and the smell of the wind itself, cleansed by a midday rain or scented with the piñon pine.

The air is precious to the red man, for all things share the same breath – the beast, the tree, the man, they all share the same breath. The white man does not seem to notice the air he breathes. Like a man dying for many days, he is numb to the stench. But if we sell you our land, you must remember that the air is precious to us, that the air shares its spirit with all the life it supports. The wind that gave our grandfather his first breath also receives his last sigh. And the wind must also give our children the spirit of life. And if we sell you our land, you must keep it apart and sacred, as a place where even the white man can go to taste the wind that is sweetened by the meadow's flowers.

So we will consider your offer to buy the land. If we decide to accept, I will make one condition: the white man must treat the beasts of this land as his brothers.

I am a savage and I do not understand any other way. I have seen a thousand rotting buffalos on the prairie, left by the white man who shot them from a passing train. I am a savage and I do not understand how the smoking iron horse can be more important than the buffalo that we kill only to stay alive.

What is man without the beasts? If all the beasts were gone, men would die from a great loneliness of the spirit. For whatever happens to the beasts soon happens to the man. All things are connected.

You must teach your children that the ground beneath their feet is the ashes of our grandfathers. So that they will respect the land, tell your children that the Earth is rich with the lives of our kin. Teach your children, that the Earth is our mother. Whatever befalls the Earth befalls the sons of the Earth. If men spit upon the ground, they spit upon themselves.

This we know: the Earth does not belong to man; man belongs to the Earth. This we know. All things are connected like the blood which unites one family. All things are connected.

Whatever befalls the Earth befalls the sons of the Earth. Man does not weave the web of life, he is merely a strand in it. Whatever he does to the web, he does to himself.

But we will consider your offer to go to the reservation you have for my people. We will live apart, and in peace. It matters little where we spend the rest of our days. Our children have seen their fathers humbled in defeat. Our warriors have felt shame, and after defeat they turn their days in idleness and contaminate their bodies with sweet foods and strong drink. It matters little where we spend the rest of our days. They are not many. A few more hours, a few more winters, and none of the children of the great tribes that once lived on this Earth or that roam now in small bands in the woods will be left to mourn the graves of the people once as powerful and as hopeful as yours. But why should I mourn the passing of my people? Tribes are made of men, nothing more. Men come and go, like the waves of the sea.

Even the white man whose God walks and talks with him as friend to friend, cannot be exempt from the common destiny. We may be brothers after all; we shall see. One thing we know, which the white man may one day discover – our God is the same God. You may think now that you own Him as you wish to own our land, but you cannot. He is the God of man and His compassion is equal for the red man and the white. This earth is precious to Him and to harm the Earth is to heap contempt on its Creator. The whites too shall pass – perhaps sooner than all other tribes.

But in your perishing you will shine brightly, fired by the strength of the God who brought you to this land and for some special purpose gave you dominion over this land and over the red man. That destiny is a mystery for us, for we do not understand when the buffalo are slaughtered, the wild horses are tamed, the secret corners of the forest heavy with the scent of many men and the view of the ripe hills blotted by talking wires.

Where is the thicket? Gone. Where is the eagle? Gone. And what is it to say goodbye to the swift pony and the hunt? The end of living and the beginning of survival.

So we will consider your offer to buy our land. If we agree it will be to secure the reservation you have promised. There, perhaps, we may live out our brief days as we wish. When the last red man has vanished from this Earth, and his memory is only the shadow of a cloud moving across the prairie, those shores and forests will still hold the spirits of my people. For they love this Earth as the new-born loves its mother's heartbeat. So if we sell you our land, love it as we've loved it. Care for it as we've cared for it. Hold in your mind the memory of the land as it was when you take it. And with all your strength, with all your mind, with all your heart, preserve it for your children and love it . . . as God loves us all.

One thing we know. Our God is the same God. This Earth is precious to Him. Even the white man cannot be exempt from the common destiny. We may be brothers after all. We shall see.

NOTES

Chapter 2
1. For further reading see Ella Elizabeth Clark, *Indian Legends of Canada*. Versions of this story are widely found among Iroquois, Huron and other First Nations.
2. For further reading see Laviolette, *The Dakota Sioux in Canada* (p. 25), and Lame Deer and Erodes, *Gift of Power* (pp. 260–5).
3. Almost identical myths of emergence are found among the Navajo, Hopi and Zuni Peoples. Zuni men in particular devote years of their lives to learning the stories of origin – 'that which was the beginning', which are formally recited once every four or eight years.

Chapter 10
1. Rudolf Kaiser, 'Chief Seattle's Speech(es): American origins and European reception', pp. 497–536, in *Recovering the Word: Essays on Native American Literature*, ed. Brian Swann and Arnold Krupat. University of California Press, 1987.

REFERENCES

Berneshawi, Suzie (1994) 'Netukulimk – resource management and the involvement of the Mi'kmaq Nation'. Unpublished Master's thesis, Dalhousie University.

Black Elk Speaks (1988) *Being the Life Story of a Holy Man of the Oglala Sioux*, as told through John G. Neihardt (first published 1932). Lincoln: University of Nebraska Press.

Bordewich, Fergus M. (1996) *Killing the White Man's Indian: Reinventing Native Americans at the End of the Twentieth Century*. New York and London: Anchor Books, Doubleday.

Brown, Jennifer S. H. and Brightman, Robert (1988) *The Orders of the Dreamed: George Nelson on Cree and Northern Ojibwa Religion and Myth, 1823*. Winnipeg: University of Manitoba Press.

Brown, Jennifer S. H. and Matthews, Maureen (1994) 'Fair wind: medicine and consolation on the Berens River', *Journal of the Canadian Historical Association*, Vol. 4, pp. 55–74.

Brown, Joseph Epes (ed.) (1953) *The Sacred Pipe: Black Elk's Account of the Seven Rites of the Oglala Sioux*. Norman: University of Oklahoma Press.

Brown, Joseph Epes (1982) *The Spiritual Legacy of the American Indian*. New York: Crossroad.

Callicott, J. B. (1989) *In Defense of the Land Ethic: Essays in Environmental Philosophy*. Albany: State University of New York.

Carlson, J. B. and Sacha, B. (1990) 'America's ancient skywatchers', *National Geographic*, March, pp. 76–107.

Clark, Ella Elizabeth (1960) *Indian Legends of Canada*. Toronto: McClelland and Stewart Limited.

Clarkson, Linda, Morrissette, Vern and Regallet, Gabriel (1992) *Our Responsibility to the Seventh Generation: Indigenous Peoples and Sustainable Development*. Winnipeg: International Institute for Sustainable Development.

Clifton, J. A. (1990) *The Invented Indian: Cultural Fictions and Government Policies*. New Brunswick and London: Transaction Publishers.

Francis, Daniel (1992) *The Imaginary Indian: The Image of the Indian in Canadian Culture*. Vancouver: Arsenal Pulp Press.

Gill, Sam D. (1983) *Native American Traditions: Sources and Interpretations*. Belmont, California: Wadsworth.

Gill, Sam D. (1987) *Mother Earth: An American Story*. Chicago and London: University of Chicago Press.

Gill, Sam D. and Sullivan, Irene F. (1992) *Dictionary of Native American Mythology*. Oxford/Denver/Santa Barbara: ABC-CLIO.

Hallowell, Alfred Irving and Brown, Jennifer S. H. (1992) *The Ojibwa of Berens River, Manitoba: Ethnography into History*. Fort Worth: Harcourt Brace Jovanovich College Publishers.

Hughes, A. et al. (1993) 'Mapping wildlife areas in the Mushkegowuk Region Cree – James Bay – N. Ontario'. Unpublished paper.

Indigenous Network Conference and Plenty Canada (December 1991) 'Indigenous Peoples' perspectives on international development and the environment', prepared for the Non-Government Organizations Conference on Environment and Development. Paris: unpublished paper.

Inglis, J. T. (ed.) (1993) *Concepts and Cases: Traditional Ecological Knowledge*. Ottawa: International Program on Traditional Ecological Knowledge, Canadian Museum of Nature.

Jacobs, Laverne. Personal correspondence.

Jenness, Diamond (1932) *The Indians of Canada* (1st edition). Ottawa: National Museums of Canada, Bulletin 65.

Johnson, M. (1992) 'Documenting Dene traditional ecological knowledge', *Akwe:kon Journal*, Summer, pp. 72–9.

Jonaitis, Aldona (ed.) (1991) *Chiefly Feasts: The Enduring Kwakiutl Potlatch*. Vancouver: Douglas and McIntyre/The American Museum of Natural History.

Kaiser, Rudolf (1987) 'Chief Seattle's Speech(es): American origins and European reception' in *Recovering the Word: Essays on Native American*

Literature, ed. Brian Swann and Arnold Krupat. Berkeley: University of California Press.

Kolondy, Annette (1975) *The Lay of the Land: Metaphor as Experience and History in American Life and Letters*. Chapel Hill: University of North Carolina Press,

Korp, Maureen (1990) 'Before Mother Earth: the Amerindian earth mound', *Studies in Religion/Sciences Religieuses*, 19/1, pp. 17–25.

Korp, Maureen (1995) 'To speak of the Earth', excerpts from *Buffalo and Garden: The Contemporary Artist's Sacred Landscape*, in press.

La Duke, Winona (1992) 'Indigenous environmental perspectives', *Akwe:kon Journal*, Summer, pp. 52–71.

Lame Deer, A. F. and Erodes, R. (1992) *Gifts of Power: The Life and Teachings of a Lakota Medicine Man*. Santa Fe: Bear & Company, pp. 260–5.

Laviolette, G. (1991) *The Dakota Sioux in Canada*. Winnipeg: DLM Publications.

McGaa, Ed (Eagle Man) (1990) *Mother Earth Spirituality: Native American Paths to Healing Ourselves and our World*. Toronto: Harper.

McKay, Revd Dr Stan (1988) 'Mending the Sacred Hoop'. Unpublished paper presented to the World Council of Churches at São Paulo, Brazil.

Manitopes, Alvin Dave Jr, Courchene, Orianna *et al.* (1992) *Voice of the Eagle: The Final Warning Message of the Indigenous People of Turtle Island Presented to the People of Mother Earth*. Earth Summit, Rio de Janeiro, June 1992. Calgary: The Aboriginal Awareness Society.

Marshall, Murdena (undated) 'Values, customs and traditions of the Mi'kmaq Nation'. Unpublished paper.

Micmac News (Union of Nova Scotia Indians monthly paper), 8 August 1978. Sydney: The Native Communications Society of Nova Scotia.

Moquin, Wayne and Van Doren, Charles (eds) (1973) *Great Documents in American Indian History*. New York: Praeger Publishers.

Morrison, Alvin H. (1982) 'The Spirit of the Law versus the Storm Spirit: a Wabanaki case' in *Papers of the Thirteenth Algonquian Conference*, ed. W. Cowan. Ottawa: Carleton University.

Old Person, Earl (1966) 'Testimony against proposed Congressional legislation' in Moquin and Van Doren, pp. 351–4.

Pleine Terre, journal publié par le Conseil culturel d'action positive, C.P. 125, succursale Beaubien, Montréal, Québec, H2G 3C8

Prins, Harald E. L. (1994) 'Neo-traditions in Native communities: Sweat Lodge and Sun Dance among the Micmac today' in *Actes du Vingt-cinquième congrès des Algonquinistes*, ed. W. Cowan. Ottawa: Carleton University.

R.D. (*Reader's Digest*) (1978) *America's Fascinating Indian Heritage: The First Americans: Their Customs, Art, History and How They Lived*. The Reader's Digest Assoc., Inc., p. 416.

Reid, Bill and Bringhurst, Robert (1984) *The Raven Steals the Light*. Vancouver: Douglas and McIntyre.

Report of the Royal Commission on Aboriginal Peoples, October 1996. Ottawa, five volumes.

Robinson, Eric and Quinney, Henty Bird (1985) *The Infested Blanket: Canada's Constitution – Genocide of Indian Nations*. Winnipeg: Queenston House Publishing.

Solidarité, quarterly newsletter of Aboriginal Rights Coalition, Ottawa.

Speck, F. G. (1915) 'Family hunting territories and social life', *American Anthropologist*, Spring.

Speck, F. K. (1977) 'Animals in special relation to man' in *Naskapi: The Savage Hunters of the Labrador Peninsula*. Norman: University of Oklahoma Press.

Tanner, A. (1979) 'Ritual relations between hunters and game animals killed' in *Bringing Home the Animals*. London: C. Hurst and Co.

Teit, J. A. (1906) *The Jesup North American Expedition*, Vol. II. Part V – *The Lillooet Indians*, ed. F. Boas. New York: G. E. Stechert.

Tinker, George (1992) 'The full circle of liberation', *Sojourners*, October, pp. 12–17. Washington: Sojourners Resource Centre, Box 29272.

Versluis, Arthur (1994) *Native American Traditions*. Shaftesbury, Dorset/Rockport, Massachusetts/Brisbane: Element.

Wright, Ronald (1993) *Stolen Continents: The New World through Indian Eyes*. London: Penguin Books.

Yellowtail, T. and Fitzgerald, M. O. (1991) *Yellowtail: Crow Medicine Man and Sun Dance Chief, an Autobiography*. Norman: University of Oklahoma Press.

Young, D., Ingram, G. and Swartz, L. (1989) *Cry of the Eagle*. Toronto: University of Toronto Press.

BANNOCK
A traditional First Nations food

Ever since the time of the early fur traders, who carried their supplies with them by canoe across Canada, bannock has been a favourite dish of First Nations People. It is invariably sold at pow-wows, and local 'Indian Days' celebrations on reserves. Originally it would have been cooked on the long-handled iron skillet held over a camp fire, and is still cooked this way by campers, or trappers out in the bush. More frequently today it is cooked at home in the oven of an electric stove.

Ingredients:
- 3¾ cups of flour
- 4½ tablespoons of white sugar (this is optional)
- ¾ teaspoon salt
- 7½ teaspoons baking powder
- 4½ tablespoons of oil or margarine
- 1½ cups of water

Mix the dry ingredients first, then add the oil and water. Knead the dough on a floured board for quite a long time, until the bannock falls away from the hands. Then roll out on a floured surface to about two inches (5 cm) thick, and place on a flat cookie sheet.

Cook in the oven at 400–450°F for about 20 minutes, or until golden brown on top. It can be cooked on a camp fire, by placing the rolled-out bannock in a well-greased skillet or iron frying pan and holding over the fire, but take care to cook it slowly, to ensure that the centre is well cooked without burning the bottom.

Place on a rack to cool with a clean cloth over the top to prevent it hardening too fast.

Variations: You can add whatever wild berries are available, such as blueberries, Saskatoon berries etc., or half a cup of raisins, or grated cheese etc.